LIFE BY THE HOUR

All scripture quotations, unless otherwise indicated, are taken
from the HOLY BIBLE, TODAY'S NEW INTERNATIONAL VERSION®. TNIV®.
Copyright © 2001, 2005 by International Bible Society.
Used by permission of Zondervan

Most Trafford titles are also available at major online book retailers.

Note for Librarians: A cataloguing record for this book is available from Library
and Archives Canada at www.collectionscanada.ca/amicus/index-e.html

Printed in Victoria, BC, Canada.

ISBN: 978-1-4269-1152-1 (soft cover)
ISBN: 978-1-4269-1154-5 (eBook)

*We at Trafford believe that it is the responsibility of us all, as both individuals
and corporations, to make choices that are environmentally and socially sound.
You, in turn, are supporting this responsible conduct each time you purchase a
Trafford book, or make use of our publishing services. To find out how you are
helping, please visit www.trafford.com/responsiblepublishing.html*

*Our mission is to efficiently provide the world's finest, most comprehensive
book publishing service, enabling every author to experience success.
To find out how to publish your book, your way, and have it available
worldwide, visit us online at www.trafford.com*

Trafford rev. 6/25/2009

 www.trafford.com

North America & international
toll-free: 1 888 232 4444 (USA & Canada)
phone: 250 383 6864 ♦ fax: 250 383 6804 ♦ email: info@trafford.com

ACKNOWLEDGMENTS

A list of those who have impacted me to the extent that their thoughts are reflected in these pages would be longer than the book itself. I have been richly blessed! Some individuals, however, must be mentioned.

I was raised in a very practical, "Life By The Hour" family by parents who endeavored to live each moment obedient to their God. What a gift! For a number of years I've been privileged to call Bill Hybels a friend. He has challenged me to higher levels each time I've been with him. Roberta Sawatsky's editing skill and insightful "question asking" ability has been invaluable. Ron Schlitt has been the friend who asked me every week, "How's the book coming?" and who assisted the progress at every turn. Joined by Brian Wall over many coffee discussions he's been the driving force behind this book.

Of course, my three loves are my constant inspiration. Arlene, Lindsey (and Chris) and Travis. No one is more blessed than me!

Contents

PART III COMMON INVESTMENT PITFALLS

PART IV SURVIVAL STRATEGIES

PART V DON'T JUST SURVIVE—FLOURISH

Introduction

People write books for people. Occasionally, however, one needs to pause and ask, "For which people?" Clearly, only God can write something for everyone, so who, specifically, am I writing for?

It was my quest to answer that question that resulted in something far more valuable than the completion of this book. I was led down a path which explored not only who I'm writing for but why I am writing at all.

It was during the process of struggling through those questions that a phenomenon occurred which I call a Divine Convergence. In a rare moment of clarity, I found unity and purpose in a number of arenas of my life which I previously viewed as disjointed. My life passion receives its fuel from being a bridge or an arc between the Timeless Truths of God and Present Day People. I am most fully alive in those moments when I see the "light go on" and people in my network of influence get the connection between what God has been saying all along and life as they experience it. It doesn't matter whether that takes place through a talk I give, an article I write or a conversation about fitness or the criminal justice system over coffee. It's all about that connection between timeless truth and modern life.

Which brings me to this book. If you have life pretty much figured out, if your theology is decided with most of the i's dotted and the t's crossed, if your expectation of an author is someone who can resonate with your incredible spiritual depth, then please skip this book, it's not for you. This book is written for people like me who struggle with knowing how to live the next half hour consistent with the truth I understand. It's written for my friends who don't go to church or read the Bible but who wonder if there is some truth in Christianity they're missing. It's written for sincere Christ-followers who are looking for a starting point for conversations about life and faith with people they love. If that's you – happy reading and I pray for a convergence between eternity and this present moment in your life.

PART ONE
Investing By The Hour

CHAPTER ONE
Survive And Flourish

Surviving

"Therefore do not worry about tomorrow,
for tomorrow will worry about itself.
Each day has enough trouble of its own." (Jesus Christ)

Boy is that an understatement! I've never stopped part way through the day and thought to myself, " All this day really needs is a bit more trouble." Have you?

As we pulled to a stop in front of the house nothing appeared out of the ordinary. I'd spent almost ten years as an Auxiliary Constable with the Royal Canadian Mounted Police and had attended hundreds of calls just like it.

"Three-Bravo-Nine, Control," our radio chirped, "Copy a complaint of a distraught female." The call could involve anything from a lost cat to an obscene phone call to a fight with her husband.

She met us in the driveway, visibly upset. All she could do was point to the garage and mumble, "He's in there." After several unsuccessful attempts to gain more information, my partner and I cautiously opened the garage door and peered inside. He was in there alright, her twenty-something-year-old boyfriend, with a rope around his neck, the other end firmly attached to the rafters.

It was not the first suicide I attended as an Auxiliary Constable and Police Chaplain, nor the last, but it was one of the most vivid. Holding the lifeless body while my partner cut the rope etched a memory so deep in me it won't soon, if ever, disappear.

Later that night, as I went off shift, and many times since, I've been plagued by the memory of that scene. I've wondered, "What could possibly have been so overwhelming in the life of that young man to lead him to such drastic, irrevocable action?" The experience raises several questions:

- What factors make life unlivable?
- Is there an anti-dote?
- Is there a secret formula to survival?

Hold those questions for a few minutes while we check out the other end of the spectrum.

Flourishing

*"I have come that they may have life, and
have it to the full." (Jesus Christ)*

I stood humbly at Oscar's bed, his death bed. He'd been a life-long family friend. I'd looked up to and admired Oscar since my youth and knew that my dad loved him like a brother. As his illness progressed his family put his bed in the living room so he could more readily visit with the constant stream of people coming to see him. On the day of his death, a fellow pastor and I visited Oscar, an 80-year-old welder. We thanked him for his unparalleled example of living a full and meaningful life, prayed with him and prepared to leave. Although he was so weak he could barely talk, he stopped us. We had prayed, but he hadn't and he wanted to. We bowed our heads again as this man, hours before his departure from earth, led in a powerful prayer of gratefulness for all the blessings he had and continued to enjoy. There was no regret, no bitterness, not even any wistfulness or wishful thinking, just gratitude. We left his home with tears streaming down our cheeks. We knew we had just been in the presence of the sacred. We had witnessed someone who had learned the key to maximum living. Like my experience in the garage, my experience with Oscar raised similar questions

- How does this kind of life happen?

- Is there a secret formula?

- How does one come to the end of life in total peace, knowing they have accomplished their God-sanctioned purpose?

- Could the young man in the garage have learned anything from Oscar about how to not only survive but flourish?

Bridging The Gap

This book was born from the need to bridge the gap between my experience on a police call that night in the garage and my experience that special afternoon beside Oscar's bed. The more I questioned the gap, the more pressing it became to close it. As I struggled, two questions emerged. I suspect it's a rare week they don't cross your mind, either consciously or in your sub-conscious.

The first question appears on tough days when you're in over your head. You may phrase it differently but in your own way you wonder, "How can I keep from being overwhelmed by the pressures and complexities in my life?" Asking that launches you into all kinds of connected issues. You begin to wonder if life has ever been as tough for anyone else and whether the pressure is survivable.

The second question typically emerges on good days when times are more relaxed. It rises to the surface during moments of reflection and introspection when things are going well. "How can I experience the maximum life has to offer?" you wonder. This question too has some cousins. "How can I flourish and make the most out of my life?" "Will I miss out on the very best God has in mind for me?"

Two piercing questions captured by two words: Surviving and Flourishing. Two words deeply embedded in the nitty, gritty struggle of life. Can I make it, and will I flourish?

Volumes have been written on this topic, many of them remarkably helpful. So why add to the pile? Because the purpose of this book is different! I have no intention to argue the meaning of life. My only intent is to apply it. I am convinced that others have done a superior job wrestling with and declaring the truth about life. The problem is that many of us haven't learned how to access that truth and meaningfully appropriate it into our daily or hourly routines.

I suspect my own journey is typical and may help clarify the goal. In my own attempt to make sense out of life I turned to a number of authors and found their work stimulating and helpful. In the mid-nineties Bob Buford wrote his legendary book, <u>Half Time</u>. He challenged middle-aged people to figure out what one thing was worth devoting the second half of life to. It was both a provocative and insightful treatment for middle-aged doldrums. About the same time, Laurie Beth Jones wrote <u>The Path</u>, a book designed to help people gain clarity on their personal life mission. Both <u>Half Time</u> and <u>The Path</u> became core curriculum for small groups all around North America, challenging those of us stuck in the humdrum of "just existing" or "earning a living" to gain an exciting sense of life's purpose and mission. "Clarify your personal mission statement," they said, "and then arrange your life around it." It was great counsel, especially when the mission you embrace is connected to a clear understanding of the Creator's plan for you and not just your own self-focused greed. Both books motivated and challenged me immeasurably. Unfortunately, they also left me one step short.

Then, in the early 2000's, the best seller from the pen of Rick Warren arrived, <u>Purpose Driven Life</u>. It's tough to find fault with a product that has encouraged more than twenty-five million people to discover their God-given purpose, especially when the purpose proposed is not the usual navel-gazing fluff but a strong directive toward the substantive goals of worshipping God and serving others. With <u>Purpose Driven Life</u> applauded by everyone from Larry King to Billy Graham, I'm sure Rick wasn't laying awake nights waiting for my approval, however, how can I not join the grateful crowd? His book was helpful to change the trajectories of countless thousands of lives, including mine. Unfortunately, or perhaps fortunately, it too left me wanting the next step. My life purpose was clear; I just kept falling short of it. One question I kept asking myself was, "How do I get <u>Half Time</u>, <u>The Path</u>, <u>Purpose Driven Life</u>, or far more important, <u>The Holy Bible</u>, out of the realm of great theory, and into my daily practice?" If I had met the young man in the garage one day sooner, would I have had an approach to life to offer him that would have enabled him to navigate the critical next 24 hours? What is it that gets us through those moments of desperation or emptiness? Or, in addition to the desperate moments, what is it that adds meaning and fullness when life is going well?

The answer to this challenge is learning to live **Life By The Hour!** Surviving and flourishing are both hourly pursuits not one time battles which, once won, last a lifetime.

Defining The Issue

The core issue of both surviving and flourishing is this: most of us bog down long before we attain the grand ideal of purpose-driven or mission-oriented lives. As grateful as I am to those who have demonstrated the power of uncovering and unleashing concepts that grandiose, I've discovered my struggle, and the struggle of many ordinary people like me, isn't typically with the big picture of life, it's managing to get to lunch time without doing something to screw it up.

I've found I need help, not so much with my life purpose as I do with living the next hour consistent with that purpose.

It was Jesus Christ who instructed His followers, "Therefore, do not worry about tomorrow, for tomorrow will worry about itself. Each day has enough trouble of its own." (Matt. 6:34) The secret to victorious living is not finding a magical key to unlock your whole future. The secret is to unlock the next hour and then the next and then the one after that. One at a time.

The freedom most of us need is freedom from the pressure to successfully live our whole life today! There is just one job for today and that's to live today. Not tomorrow, not next week, and not next year. In fact, sometimes, living even one day is too big a challenge. The next hour is all we can manage. So, how about focusing on just one hour? One hour! Don't try to survive it. You can do better than that. Flourish! Live it to the max, live it to the extreme, in alignment

> *I've found I need help, not so much with my life purpose as I do with living the next hour consistent with that purpose.*

with your God-given calling. Is that doable? Absolutely – after all, it's only an hour!! And if you can do it this hour, what's to keep you from doing it next hour and the one after that?

This book doesn't pretend to be a solution to all life's challenges. What it is, is a way of thinking about life. But once you catch the principle, the applications have no boundaries.

Stop The Clock

1. *We all have life goals that have never been realized. That's reality! Identify some of those goals in your life and list the obstacles that prevented you from achieving them.*

2. *Have you experienced a "Divine Convergence?" Describe the circumstances around that discovery. How did it impact you?*

3. *Do you have a tendency to try to live "too much life at a time? What lessons have you learned that keep you from giving in to that tendency?*

CHAPTER TWO
Believe The Strategy

10 + 1 may not equal 11. It may equal success!

The day Life By The Hour became real to me had nothing to do with overwhelming issues such as career choice or marriage. It had to do with exercise. I took up running, marathon running.

(If you'll allow me to boast just a bit, I recently completed my 13th marathon, a goal previously unthinkable to me. To celebrate the moment my wife presented me with a beautiful 26.2 ring).

I didn't have history as a runner and had no coach. I simply bought a book about marathon running, read it and tried to do what it said. I found it overwhelming, especially when approaching 3 or 3½ hour training runs. How does anyone run for 3½ hours? Normal people don't! Neither do those who are sane. Ready to quit in despair I stumbled (almost literally) across a runner who trained differently. He followed a program created by

Olympian Jeff Galloway and a Canadian named John Stanton, founder of The Running Room chain of stores. They didn't set out to develop a program for Olympic athletes but rather to help ordinary people like me run marathons. The secret: 10 & 1. Run 10 minutes then walk for 1. Run 10 more, and walk 1. Just do it over and over (and over and over) again. It was revolutionary and unbelievably liberating! I didn't have to set out to run for 3 hours, just for the next 10 minutes. I quit telling myself I had 30 more kilometers to run, just 10 more minutes. I began to discover that A VERY BIG TASK BECAME DOABLE!!!

I wonder if it would have made a difference if the young man in the garage had known that life could be lived an hour, or even just 10 minutes at a time. As I write these words I wonder what difference it will make if you choose to believe it, embrace it and put it into practice.

Life by the hour is not a new concept, just a forgotten one. 2000 years ago Jesus said, "Whoever can be trusted with very little can also be trusted with much and whoever is dishonest with very little will also be dishonest with much." (Luke 16:10) The battle isn't about mastering the huge decisions of life that are suddenly thrust on you. The battle is won or lost in the small choices along the way. They equip you for the big ones.

William James, a pioneer in philosophy and psychology, said, "All of life is but a mass of small choices – practical, emotional and intellectual – systematically organized for our greatness or grief." When asked if these choices could be altered, he replied, "Yes, one at a time. But we must never forget that it's not only our big dreams that shape reality ….The small choices bear us irresistibly toward our destiny." (cited in Cooper, p. xvi)

Dr. Robert Cooper declares that, "A distinctive, learning-filled life results from a succession of small, specific choices made each day." (Cooper, p. 7)

I cite these sources not because this is an academic treatment in which the one with the most footnotes gets an A, but because I long for you to understand that the principle of hourly living is a time-tested, Bible-based truth that in our rapid-fire, "quick-get-me-to-the-goal" mindset we have ignored.

We've accepted the model and practice it in many other areas of life, just not where it matters most. At the risk of being ridiculous, let me point out that no one attempts to eat an entire week's nutrition, at one sitting. We are designed to eat a little bit at a time and surprising to no one, the more we learn about our bodies the more we are discovering that the system of three square meals a day we were raised to believe was healthy is far from the ideal. Most nutritional experts today promote the practice of grazing, eating 5, 6 or even more, small meals a day.

We not only eat in manageable portions, we also work best in short energy bursts. No one arrives at work and explodes for 8 or 10 hours. Rather, we break each day into manageable segments. We design projects to be attacked before morning coffee break, between coffee and lunch, early afternoon, after the afternoon coffee break and so on. We've learned that smaller, more manageable chunks of time are unquestionably the most productive.

It's not by accident that Network television uses the same concept, especially when broadcasting lengthy events like the Olympic Games. Their programmers understand that the way to entice the world to stay tuned for hours is to capture each seven minute segment.

The Foundational Principle

The foundational principle of Life By The Hour is gleaned from the ancient story of the Exodus found in the Older Testament of the Bible. If you possess even a cursory knowledge of the Bible you'll recognize the Exodus as a pivotal event not only in biblical history but in world history. Thanks to Hollywood even if you're unfamiliar with the Bible you'll know enough of this account to recognize its relevance.

The Setting: An entire nation of people was trapped, not just in a meaningless existence but in a horrendous one.

Put yourself in their place, living in slavery, no chance to better yourself and no hope for your children's future. In fact, things are so bad your baby boys are being murdered and your baby girls are at constant risk of being violated. Into that depressing existence comes something you've not felt for a long, long time – hope! There's a promise from God that you can leave Egypt. Eagerly you pack up your family with the dream of a new future.

Does this story contain any parallels to life as you know it? Are you reading this book because somewhere deep inside you is a hope that life can be different than the way you've been experiencing it?

Part of the beauty of history is that if we have the eyes to see them, there are constant parallels which can inform the present. Few of us experience life quite as low as the Israelites in captivity, but that doesn't mean we don't know about lows. Nor does it mean we don't understand full well the riveting chains of slavery. If you can't identify with survival challenges today, it's only a matter of time, at some point they'll come. But what will also come, deep inside, is the God-given hope that you can survive, that life can be different. Part of the created essence of our lives is the belief that misery, mediocrity and meaninglessness can be left behind.

Deep within us all is the hope that there is a promised land.

Purpose-filled living is not a mirage. The question is, "How do we turn that hope into reality?"

Let's return to the story. No sconer had the Israelites left Egypt than they encountered the Red Sea. Bummer! So much for the myth that getting to the Promised Land would be easy. But, with God's help they faced the Red Sea project – and won. That experience gave birth to a second essential quality: faith. First they experienced hope that life could be different and now faith was born, causing them to believe that God could help them overcome the obstacles between them and a new life.

Stop reading for a moment and process what's just been said. Let me repeat it: Two essential qualities are *hope* that your life can be different and *faith* that God can help you overcome the obstacles you will (will, not may), face en route.

> Deep within us all is the hope that there is a promised land.

Back to the story, the next movement is crucial! The next movement could change your life! The next movement is the foundation of Life By The Hour! Pay very, very close attention.

They ran out of food. They lacked the resources to make it to the Promised Land. And it's only a matter of time until it happens to you. Everyone, sooner or later arrives at exactly that point. You have a dream that life can get better, you believe God is calling you to it, He's even helped you overcome a few obstacles along the way, but suddenly you run out of "everything," food, drive, faith, support and ultimately, hope.

It's true isn't it? You've experienced it? I have.

What they needed now was a PLAN to help them cope with reality..

In those valleys of life the first thing to go is perspective. Let me quit writing and direct you to the actual, historical account because no one can tell it better than the Scripture writer. *"The Israelites said to them (Moses and Aaron), 'If only we had died by the Lord's hand in Egypt! There we sat around pots of meat and ate all the food we wanted, but you have brought us out into this desert to starve this entire assembly to death.'" (Exodus 16:3)* Who were they kidding? Did any of them actually view Egypt as "the good old days?" When a dream dies, it's amazing how enticing your past can appear. You forget to ask yourself, "Why did I ever dream life could be different in the first place if it was so good back then?" My last job, my last spouse, my singleness, my childlessness, just fill in the blank ... Problems lead most of us to lose focus and perspective on reality.

It's at this point God unfolds the strategy! He'd already given them hope. He'd already proved He could be trusted. What they needed now was a PLAN to help them cope with reality. The plan God presented was living life one day at a time!

*"Then the Lord said to Moses, 'I will rain down bread from heaven for you. The people are to go out **each day** and gather enough **for that day**. In this way I will test them and see whether they will follow my instructions.'" (Exodus 16:4)*

Each day! Gather enough for THAT day!! Face the present need. You'll be given enough supply for this moment, not for the whole journey, not for your whole life. Try to gather more and it'll just turn to mold. Life is intended to be lived step by step, moment by moment, hand in hand with God. That's faith! It takes a lot of trust to live one day or one hour at a time but it's there, in each hour that you find the power both to survive and to flourish!

Stop The Clock

1. *Have you ever found yourself referring to the "good ole days?" What made them so good? Were they really that good? Once you pause to consider it, is your perspective accurate?*

2. *What's going on in your life currently that makes you wish for times past?*

3. *Do you really want to go back, or is your real desire to move forward?*

The point was clearly made that moving forward involves a plan. Within the next 24 hours what is one step you can take to move you forward? Who or what do you need to help you take that step? Are you willing to ask for the help?

CHAPTER THREE

Training To Invest

The way you train is the way you'll die ...
or the way you'll live.

Several years into my work with the RCMP Auxiliary I accepted the invitation to become a firearms instructor. The very idea of a minister teaching people to shoot isn't the norm but who says you need to follow the norm? The training we received as instructors was some of the most valuable to which I've ever been exposed. Training others in the use of lethal force requires you to accept that there is no room for error in your instruction, none. Every lecture, training technique, dry fire and firing line you oversee needs to be carried out with flawless precision. The mantra our instructors recited to us, over and over again was, "The way you train is the way you die." They told stories and showed video of police officers who died for no reason other than poor training. One account I found particularly compelling described police officers who died holding the brass from spent cartridges in their hands. In the days of the revolver, before the semi-automatic pistol became the norm, we all used the old six-shot revolver. After shooting six rounds, you would empty the brass from the cylinder and re-load. However, since brass was re-useable, and firing ranges had to be kept clean, lazy instructors allowed lazy shooters to empty the spent brass into their hands instead of quickly dumping it onto the ground and re-loading. Empty cartridges could easily be tossed into a pail and the grounds would be clean at the end of the training session. Hundreds of officers trained that way. They were more focused on not having to pick up brass from the ground than they were on re-loading quickly. The tragedy was that investigations into the shootings of police officers revealed that numbers of them died clutching empty brass in their hands.

When the moment comes, the way you practice IS the way you die, or the way you live. The way you manage life's little encounters is the way you'll face the "biggies."

Jesus told a story about a man who decided to go on a journey and entrusted his possessions to his employees. He didn't give them all the same amount but divided his portfolio according to their ability. Probably as he suspected, upon his return he discovered that some of his employees proved more faithful than others, leading to the classic principle of Matthew 25:23 *"...you have been faithful with a few things; I will put you in charge of many things."*

No one questions the importance of making right choices when big decision times arrive. Career choices, marital choices, choices about whether or not to have children and decisions concerning major financial purchases all rank high on the scale of "making sure you get it right." Rarely, however, do we recognize that making the right choices at those major crossroads is a direct consequence of how we've trained. Right decisions in critical moments result from right decisions in every moment. Life By The Hour rests on the belief that if you are bullish on making right choices in those every day, every hour situations that aren't all that complicated or difficult, you'll make them by default when the big moments arrive. Investing in life training prepares you for the more significant performances.

One of my favorite books is the Book of Proverbs from the Older Testament of the Bible. Chapter 7 begins with this challenge: "*My son, keep my words and store up my commands within you. Keep my commands and you will live; guard my teachings as the apple of your eye. Bind them on your fingers; write them on the tablet of your heart (Proverbs 7:1-3).*"

The author, arguably the wisest man to ever live says that the key to life is to find a way to ingrain your most deeply held, God-given and God-honoring values into the fabric of your life. One way to do that, if necessary, is to tie a string around your finger. What a ludicrous thought. In today's vernacular we'd say, "Put a sticky note where you'll constantly see it or set your Outlook alarm to remind you of it every five minutes." Force yourself to be perpetually aware of your values until they become "written on your heart." Until they become a natural way of life for you.

> *Right decisions in critical moments result from right decisions in every moment.*

Simply put, Life By The Hour is a string around your finger. It's a method of encoding core values into your life by making them a constant, hourly part of your conscious decision-making, until they become habitual. In fact, the goal is to go beyond habit and, as Proverbs says, to stick with it until the practices you desire become a natural part of your sub-conscious thinking. When you have chosen the right path so frequently that it becomes instinct, you'll be ready to both survive and flourish, regardless what life throws your way.

Stop The Clock

1. *Is there anything in the way you handled a trivial disagreement with your spouse that will impact the way you handle a major marital dispute?*

2. *Are there frequent, little decisions you make professionally that are shaping the way you'll make major calls?*

3. *What is it about the way you treated the clerk who gave you incorrect change that will impact the way you negotiate a major contract?*

4. *What impact will your daily decision regarding stairs versus elevator have on your future health?*

Every decision leads to a direction and every direction leads to a destination. Train for the little decisions early.

STRATEGIC INVESTMENTS

Direction: You Gotta Know Where You're Going

It doesn't take me an hour to get off course …
I can get lost in a minute!

Most meaningful gift received: a compass with a note from
my wife saying, "I love you too much to lose you."

Several years ago my son and I set out on a wonderful father-son expedition. His baseball team was playing in the Provincial Championship Series held on Vancouver Island. The trip involved a five hour drive followed by a two hour ferry ride followed by another two hour drive.

I made a reservation for the ferry weeks in advance and when the day came, off we went. We had a great trip, arriving at the ferry terminal in time to have a picnic lunch before boarding. To show

how perfect things were, since it was just us "boys" we didn't bother to eat the crusts from our sandwiches, they went to the pigeons. Finally they called for us to board the ferry. Unbelievably, our car refused to start. In a panic I opened the hood and stood there attempting to look like I knew what I was doing. It's default mode for males to at least pretend. Unfortunately, even in my mechanical ignorance I could see that we had a major problem; we'd blown the post right out of the battery. As I stood helplessly in front of the car the guy beside us got out of his truck. He was very handy, had one of those tools on his belt that could launch a space ship, and in fact he even looked a bit like the television character, McGuyver. While we stood watching, he carefully wedged everything back in place, using tin foil from our lunch. He then boosted us and got the car started. I wish I knew his name, he was great. He then assured us that the worst case scenario would be that they might have to push us off on the other side at which point we could arrange for repairs.

Sure enough, two hours later we arrived at Nanaimo terminal and our car wouldn't start. I alerted ferry staff and they told me they'd help as soon as everyone else was unloaded. They brought their truck on board and boosted us, but to no avail. The battery post was gone, and by this time so was McGuyver. They said, "No problem, we'll push you off," and positioned their truck behind us. However, problem number two chose that moment to appear. On all newer model cars everything is electric and we didn't have enough juice to get the gear shift out of Park. By this time, they had begun to load the ferry to go back to Vancouver. We worked feverishly, but not fast enough. They loaded the entire ferry around us and off we went, two hours in the opposite direction.

Before sailing, I pleaded with the foreman to let us off to arrange for repairs, but the captain, ever security conscious said, "If his car is on this ship, so is he."

As we sailed out of view of land headed in the wrong direction, it suddenly hit me—I had about ten minutes before we'd be out of cell phone range. I either had to come up with a plan or we'd spend the rest of our lives going back and forth across the ocean.

Getting a tow truck company to purchase a new battery and starter cable and to meet us at 11:00 at night, all on the strength of a cell phone call was no easy feat but we were desperate.

Part way through our trip back to Vancouver, one of the ferry workers who'd heard of our predicament found us and said, "Meet me at your car, I know how to get it out of Park."

I said, "Great, we're on Deck 4, Stairway 4."

He just looked at me and laughed. "Sir," he said, "it won't be hard to find, it's the only car on the ship pointing the wrong direction."

They made us sit in the car while all the other vehicles unloaded in Vancouver. Every car on the ship drove by us pointing and laughing at the fools facing the wrong way. You could hear them laugh and exclaim, "How did they get on the ship backwards?" You have no idea how badly I wanted to "wave" back at them.

Finally, after our third ferry ride of the day we returned to Nanaimo to be met by a tow-truck driver who turned out to be a left over hippie wearing a t-shirt that said, "Support Your Local Police: The Best Bed and Breakfast In Town." I almost had a heart attack realizing our welfare rested in his hands. He quickly surprised me by towing our car off the boat, fixing the problem and getting us on the road again. To this day he holds shares in our house.

Let's get to the point. Other than the therapeutic value I receive each time I tell that story there is one other significant purpose: to demonstrate the absurdity of our situation. Every person I've told about our trips back and forth has exclaimed, "That's insane!" Absolutely! There's not a person alive who can't immediately see the ridiculousness of floating back and forth across the ocean, going no where. No one would tolerate that for more than the briefest moment.

Yet we tolerate it in our lives almost every day! We just do laps, with no sense of direction. We get up, go to work, come home, eat, spend ENTIRE evenings watching TV, go to bed, get up and do it all over again. And far too often we do it without ever once thinking about what we're doing. Without connecting our activity to what we believe our God-given direction or purpose is all about. We do it without asking, "Where am I going?" Routine isn't a life-killer, meaningless routine is.

Life By The Hour proposes hourly compass readings. These are not designed to be hourly crises of faith, rather 15 or 20 second reminders of your life-direction. They are designed to function like the voice on your GPS. If you've programmed your destination into your GPS it will inform you of every turn along the way. If you're aware of the direction you want your life to go:

- the glass of water you grab as you pass the cooler becomes an investment into your healthy life-style;

- the conversation at coffee becomes part of your desire to be an encouraging person;

- the prayer you breathe as you pass the work station occupied by a co-worker going through a messy divorce becomes a reflection of your desire to embrace compassion in your life.

Left unchallenged, routine tends to become meaningless, so learn to challenge it, every single hour.

Stop The Clock

1. *Predict what your day might look like if you lived it with these questions on the top of your mind each hour:*

> ➤ *Is there anything in the activity of the next hour that can help me get where I believe I need to go?*

> ➤ *Is there anything about my life I can learn from doing this next project?*

> ➤ *As I head into this coffee break is there a way I can steer conversation toward something enriching?*

> ➤ *Is there one moment of value I can take away from my daily commute?*

> ➤ *Can our family dinner tonight accomplish more than just nutrition?*

> ➤ *When I pick up the kids from school in 15 minutes is there anything I can say or do that they'll comment on at my funeral?*

Make a conscious effort to live just one day like this, and then a second day. Meet with a friend for coffee and discuss what you discover.

CHAPTER FIVE

Inspiration: The Fuel That Keeps You Going

*If life was easy, or even neutral, we wouldn't need to
be inspired. Unfortunately, that's not reality. As your
grandfather said, "It really is uphill – both ways!"*

Without question, my first marathon was my favourite.
There's something about being in uncharted waters that's particularly rewarding. As I indicated earlier, when I began training
I didn't know anything about marathon running and didn't have
a coach, I just bought a book, followed what it said and showed
up at the race. As you can imagine, I was unbelievably nervous.
What if I couldn't finish? People would ask how I did. What if I
had to tell them, "I quit part way through?"

When the gun went off I started running along with several
thousand others. It's amazing how alone you can feel in a crowd.

I kept looking around, seeing if there were any tricks I could learn from other runners. About a kilometer in I noticed a guy wearing "Rabbit Ears." I was ticked. I'd worked for months to prepare for the marathon and thought to myself, "He's making a joke of the whole thing." I was insulted. As I got closer to him I saw that he also had a sign on his back announcing that he would run the marathon in a specified time. Slowly I began to put 2+2 together. He was an official pace runner assigned by the organizers and the rabbit ears were so he would stand out among the hundreds of runners around him.

Analyzing the situation I noticed that there was a group of about 20 people running with him who seemed to be having a good time and that the sign on his back declared his marathon time was the same as my personal goal. In a split second I made a decision, the best decision of the race. I joined his group. His name was Ralph, and he was the most inspirational motivator I've ever met. First he said, "Everyone in my group is responsible for telling at least two jokes and if I were you I'd tell them now, while you can still breathe." Then he proceeded to personally encourage and compliment everyone around him.

Somewhere around the 30 kilometer mark, the first of our group members started to fade and drop out. As I observed I noticed that Ralph had a specific technique to inspire them, and we all followed his lead. First we would compliment. We'd tell struggling runners, "You're looking strong, you're looking great, come on, you can do it." It was all a total lie mind you, but we tried. When compliments didn't work, we tried challenging them with their goal. "Come on, you've worked a year for this, remember all those hard training runs? You can do this." When encouragement and challenge failed, we resorted to ridicule. One runner I'd spent the previous 25 kilometers with was a young man celebrating his first wedding anniversary, proof positive you don't need intelligence to be a marathon runner. After telling him how good he was looking and reminding him how hard he'd worked, we turned on him. I distinctly remember saying to him, "Didn't you tell me your bride is waiting for you at the finish line, thinking she married a real man? Do you want me to have to tell her the truth about you?" It worked, he sprinted ahead.

At about 34 kilometers it was my turn. My stomach was doing things it had never done, my legs were cramping, and they started in with the lies. "Oh, you're looking good." "Come on, only 8 more k to go. You've run 8 k hundreds of times."

"Sure," I muttered, "just not at the end of 34."

And then they turned on me. "You said you're a preacher, eh?" (It was a Canadian marathon). "We always knew you preachers were a bunch of wussies. That's why you couldn't get a real job."

Something inside me snapped and I blew by all of them, beating them to the finish by almost seven minutes.

The truth is, both surviving and flourishing are absolutely dependant on inspiration. In tough moments when you're ready to throw in the towel, you need to be reminded that you can make it and in great moments, you need someone or something to call out your very best. Inspiration, however, is not something that can be stored up. It's not a commodity you can receive an extra large dose of every January. It's something you need by the hour.

Hourly Doses of Inspiration

Each of us is unique. Consequently, there isn't any one, fool-proof method of inspiration that works universally. You need to discover what inspires you and take steps to put it into play in your life. It also goes without saying that variety is the spice of life. Don't count on one source of inspiration alone. Consider these time-tested inspiration booster shots.

- Scripture. Commit verses to memory that hold deep meaning to you. For example, a citation honoring my uncle who was accidentally killed at the age of 42 while a missionary in Africa, includes the verse, *"Whatever you do, work at it with all your heart as working for the Lord, and not for human masters. (Col. 3:23)."* I have the citation hanging in my den, I have that verse posted in places I'm certain to see it. I live with it as a constant inspiration to do this hour with ALL my heart. There is nothing like God's truth to inspire you, but, you have to consistently put that truth into your life.

- Encouragement. You know from past experience that there are some people who always inspire you while others drain you. You get to choose. Every day, spend a minute or two on the phone with inspiring people. Avoid the joy-vampires.

- Exercise. As often as possible I try to run at the noon hour, knowing that both the endorphins and the sense of having done something positive for myself will give me at least a 2 hour boost.

- Reverse Encouragement. I ALWAYS get a boost out of encouraging someone else. It only takes seconds to fire off an email, a brief note or a call encouraging someone and the act of inspiring others always inspires me.

- Worship. Worship is a great source of inspiration. I know I need to be careful about my motives in worship because I always want to worship because God is worthy not because I need a boost. Yet, if I'm perfectly honest, I rarely come away from worship without being inspired. Remember the Israelites and the manna? The first thing one loses in difficult times is perspective. The first thing one gains in worship is perspective. You see a God bigger than your problem, a God in control, a God Who loves you. It always changes outlook.

- Nature. Five minutes of your coffee break spent admiring a tree or flower will produce a thousand times more benefit than a second cup of coffee.

Face the fact that you are not self-sustained. You need inspiration and you need it in frequent doses. It'll help you both survive and flourish.

Stop The Clock

There are 6 inspirational suggestions on the previous pages; some may already be part of your daily routine. However, since variety is the spice of life, here's an additional challenge:

1. *Choose a different mode of inspiration each day for the next 6 days. You can do your favorite one twice!*

2. *Journal the impact each activity has on your mood, your sense of direction, your treatment of others and your closeness to God.*

3. *Have coffee (or go for a walk) with a good friend and share what you are learning about yourself. Sharing it will solidify it in your own mind.*

CHAPTER SIX

Fellowship: Life's Too Precious To Go It Alone

*I've yet to meet the person who isn't taller
when standing with a friend.*

We taught our children wrong. How many of us asked them upon the completion of their first day of school, "Did you like it?" "Did you learn anything?" "Do you like your teacher?" And, the clincher, "Did you make any friends?"

How are you supposed to make friends in one day, especially when you're not allowed to talk? Friends are the result of investment over time. They can't be quickly conjured up in moments of need or glory. They are built slowly over time. They take moment by moment, hour by hour investment.

When you choose daily to invest in friends you not only enrich their lives and your own; you prepare yourself to survive the overwhelming seasons of life and to flourish in the best times.

The ancient book of Ecclesiastes puts it this way, "*Two are better than one, because they have a good return for their labor; If they fall down, they can help each other up. But pity those who fall and have no one to help them up! Also, if two lie down together, they will keep warm. But how can one keep warm alone? Though one may be overpowered, two can defend themselves. A cord of three strands is not quickly broken.*" (Ecc. 4:9-12)

Years ago I was invited to attend a CFL playoff game. As any Canadian knows, playoff football, unless occurring in one of only two domes in the nation, is undoubtedly an adventure in snow and freezing cold. The game was between the Edmonton Eskimos and the Saskatchewan Roughriders. For half-time entertainment, there was a Jr. High School marching band from Regina. (I've never understood, the Americans get Celine Dion, we get a Jr. Hi band). Part way through the band's performance a group of young, drunk males in front of me decided it would be great fun to see if they could sink a snowball down the bell of the tuba. I have to admit, at first pass, it was kind of funny. However, what happened was totally predictable. Snow balls turned to ice balls and instead of sinking one down the tuba they began seeing if they could hit some of the young musicians. I was close enough to see tears on the faces of many of them. Watching the scene turn uglier and uglier, I finally decided to intervene. I stood up and called to the group of young drunks, "Hey, that's enough. Leave the kids alone."

They turned and looked at me and said, "Oh yeah? Who says?"

That was a pretty good question. There were 6 or 8 of them, they were young, tough and very drunk. As I struggled to come up with a meaningful answer, a great big fellow stood up behind me and said, "I say, that's who!" He was immediately followed by another, and another and another. Suddenly, filled with great courage I realized I had the answer. I said to the young men, "Yeah, I say. That's who!"

The problem hadn't changed. They were still young, tough and drunk. What had changed is that I realized I wasn't standing alone.

Who would you call if you had car trouble on a deserted stretch of road at two o'clock in the morning? If your only answer is, "A tow truck," you need to pay close attention to your friend-ship investments. Who would you call if you just received a major promotion at work? If you can't immediately think of a small group of friends who would genuinely celebrate with you, a red warning light should be flashing in your mind.

Part of your hourly investment strategy could very well include questions like:

- Who do I know who could use some encouragement from me today?

- Who do I know who could use a bit of celebration?

- Who do I have in my life who I could call tonight to hang-out, with no agenda, and still have a great time?

- How many days has it been since I've intentionally done something to help someone I care about survive or flourish?

Stop The Clock

Those are great questions so stop the clock. Don't rush past them in a hurry to get to the next hour.

1. *As you reflect on each question and your answer to it, are you satisfied with what you've answered?*

2. *Which ones sadden or challenge you?*

What relational changes do you want to implement over the course of the next few weeks?

CHAPTER SEVEN

Values: Making Sure It's Worth It

Everyone understands the importance of personal values. What they don't understand is that values never take an hour off.

Your values confront you at interesting times. In 1984 my wife, Arlene, and I had a date for lunch. It was planned to coincide with a visit to her doctor. When I saw her at the restaurant the look on her face told me all I needed to know. With tears of joy she put it into words, "It was positive," she said, "I'm pregnant!" From that moment we did everything right. Arlene adapted her diet with baby in mind. I engaged in the only truly successful construction project of my life, the development of a first class nursery. Together we read books and attended classes. This was one part of life we wanted to get right.

On December 6th, at about 3:30, she woke me with the words we'd anticipated for 9 months. "Tim," she said, "I think it's time."

I replied with the question every husband has asked since Adam. I said, "Are you sure?" How could she be "sure?" So I took out my stop watch and some graph paper and marked down not only the intervals but rated the severity of contractions. (Yes, I have been accused of being OCD).

When we were "sure," we proceeded to the hospital where a miracle happened. There are no other words to describe it. If you're a parent you know exactly what I mean. The nurse wrapped our baby girl in a blanket and said, "Mr. Schroeder, would you like to hold her?" I have no recollection of answering but I must have because moments later I looked down into the face of my little girl and that tiny baby reached out and grabbed hold of my heart with a grip I never would have believed possible. And then, to quote comedian Ken Davis, I made a fatal mistake. I blinked. And when I opened my eyes again, there I was, standing at the back of a church, my baby girl was all dressed in white, clutching my arm, and there was a strange man (who I've since learned to love) waiting down by the altar with the intent that I would turn my precious girl over to him.

If, as you read this you think I am exaggerating the speed of life, it's a sure sign that you are still very young. Anyone who's lived a while understands the uneasy feeling that accompanies each passing milestone.

Unfortunately, life does not slow down to allow you to get your value ducks in a row. Life races and your values will either be strategically integrated into each and every hour or life will pass you and your values by. The resultant tragedy is best depicted in the conclusion of one of Jesus' most popular parables, "What does it profit a man to gain the whole world yet forfeit his soul?" Imagine giving your whole life to something only to discover it is void of meaning.

No hour is neutral. It will either honor and build your values or erode them. That's why it is so critical to learn to live every hour with a values-conscious-outlook.

In the early years of computer use it was not uncommon to hear cries of anguish from friends and colleagues (and to be

> No hour is neutral. It will either honor and build your values or erode them.

fair, similar sounds resounded from my office) bemoaning the fact that hours of work had just been lost. Computer crashes in the early days were more common than not. Each time someone would lose a lot of work, the response of friends and consultants was always the same. "You mean you didn't save it?" Those early experiences taught the importance of computer settings that would automatically save work every few minutes. Today it's rare for anyone to lose more than five minutes work. We learned the value of guarding the moment. That is precisely the goal of Life By The Hour values. Don't spend a week, month, year, or God-forbid, a lifetime pursuing things that don't count. Take the time to first establish your personal values and then rehearse them with such frequency that they become second nature.

CAUTION – MISUNDERSTANDING AHEAD!!!

As you become more value conscious, let me caution you. Some people, especially well meaning Christians have assumed that honoring one's values necessitates withdrawal from society. They pull back from every expression of life that differs from their most deeply held beliefs. They live with a fear that life will pollute them. They get as far away from anything that differs from their values as is humanly possible. They home school or Christian school, play on "Christian only" sports teams, get their nails done by Christian beauticians, their hair cut by Christian stylists and their cars fixed by Christian mechanics. Believe me, I'm not anti-Christian and I'm not suggesting that any one of these practices is wrong. However, grouped together, nothing could be further from what I'm proposing. The goal of value saturation is *awareness* not *avoidance.* The goal is to instill God-honoring values so deep into your life that you are equipped to live IN this crazy, mixed up world, not in a constant attempt to escape it.

Apply a values test to everything you face. While watching television in the evening, ask questions like, "What values is that program based on?" and "How do those values compare with mine?" Rather than refusing your children participation in every activity that might contain content contrary to your values, discuss it with them. "What occurred at the party last night? How does that gel with our values?" Few possessions are more critical than a "values radar" that never takes an hour off.

Stop The Clock

1. *Think of someone you greatly admire. What values do you see lived out in his or her daily life?*

2. *Identify 3 values you aspire to live by. What changes might you want to implement in your daily activities to ensure they are reflected?*

3. *Take a risk: ask someone you trust if they see your most important values reflected in your daily living. What changes do they suggest?*

CHAPTER EIGHT

Gratitude: Investment Value – Priceless!

Of ANY investment of any amount, none pays
higher dividends than gratitude!

One Monday I visited a ticket outlet to purchase tickets to a sporting event. It seemed obvious that they weren't expecting many customers that day and had chosen to use the opportunity to train a new clerk. Within minutes of opening, however, a line-up had formed. I wish I could tell you verbatim the discussion that took place in our line but my desire to avoid profanity prohibits it. Let me just say that the discussion focused on the competence, the maternal heritage and the IQ of the novice clerk. When it was all over, I glanced at my watch and discovered the total time it took to get through the line was about four minutes.

An hour later I went for my run which began in the parking lot of the SPCA. While I was tying my shoes I saw a scene I'll not soon forget. A seriously handicapped young man in his twenties was coming up the driveway, hanging onto the leash of a Rottweiler. I learned later that together with his life-skills coach, he regularly walks dogs for the SPCA. As I watched, the dog was straining against the leash to the point where the young man was having a difficult time maintaining his balance. His physical condition made it hard for him to walk confidently at the best of times and there he was, stumbling up the driveway hanging onto a spirited dog, on the verge of toppling. The pending disaster, however, is not what caught my attention. What was captivating was the look on his face. I don't think I have ever seen a bigger smile. He just beamed, radiating joy and excitement as he staggered up that road helping an abandoned dog get some exercise.

That was Monday.

Tuesday, I sat quietly, reflecting on the previous twenty-four hours, ready to make an entry in my journal about what I had learned from the previous day. Suddenly pictures of my two Monday experiences appeared, in stark contrast. In one scene was a group of healthy, financially solid men, with discretionary time on their hands, bitterly complaining about a four minute delay in purchasing tickets to a game. In the other scene, was a young man who daily faces almost insurmountable problems, beaming with gratitude at the privilege of being able to walk a dog.

It was as if God was saying to me, "Schroeder, choose your circle." Which group do you want your life to be about?

As I explored those two circles, two Bible verses came to mind, representing the two groups. The first group was described in Numbers 11 verse 1: "*Now the people complained about their hardships in the hearing of the Lord (and get this), and when He heard them, His anger was aroused.*" It's about as direct as you can get. God apparently does not like the attitude of Group 1. Grumble, grumble, grumble. It reminds you of Goldilocks and the three bears. The porridge for some people will always be either too hot or too cold. The traffic's bad, the stock market is down, the clerk is slow, the government is a joke and your spouse snores. Grumble, grumble, grumble. Group 2 also had a verse. Philippians 4:11-12: *I have learned to be content, whatever the circumstances. I know what it is to be in need, and I know what it is to have plenty. I have learned the secret of being content in any and every situation, whether well fed or hungry, whether living in plenty or in want.* What an interesting comment! "I have learned it," says St. Paul. It doesn't come naturally. It's not just part of some peoples' personality. It is learned behavior.

I am completely convinced that one of the biggest and best investments you can make with your life is to invest in Group 2 living. BUT – you guessed it – Group 2 living doesn't happen because of one huge decision or one major investment. It happens one decision at a time, hour by hour.

Let's trace the process; there are two critical elements to it. First, understand that choosing which circle to stand in is yours, and it's yours hourly. You may have chosen the wrong circle last hour, deal with it and move on — you have a new hour in front of you! Choose to live it differently. Psalm 107 says, "O that people would give thanks to the Lord ..." Four times it repeats in that Psalm, "O that we WOULD ..." We've got the technology to do it. We've got the opportunity to do it. We've got the reason to do it. We just need to choose it.

I have a route I like to run that includes a fierce challenge. The challenge is a dog that lives on that route who loves to chase me. And I don't mean for fun. I mean, ears back, hair up, teeth bared. For about a year we've had an ongoing battle. I don't want to call

Dog Control because I figure I should be able to handle it myself. So I load up with rocks, I carry pepper spray if I know I'm going to run that route, it has become a true battle of the wills. However, I also complain about that dog to anyone who'll listen. I've actually preached about it. Recently, while complaining about the dog yet again, it hit me. I don't have to run there. Simple isn't it? There are thousands of kilometers of roads around our city where I can run, I don't have to run past that dog if I don't choose to. It is 100% my call.

So is gratitude! I don't have to get worked up about heavy traffic or slow service or the neighbor's kid with the squeaky bike... it is my choice. I can choose to find something in every hour for which to be grateful, and when I do, it changes everything.

The second critical element is to make your choice tangible. There is a big difference between just thinking a grateful thought and choosing to act on it. Every time you do something tangible in response to your gratitude it solidifies it. And it doesn't take much time. It only takes about thirty seconds to rattle off an email. It takes less than that to jot down a blessing on a sticky note to keep in front of you. It takes almost no time to keep a gratitude journal handy and jot things down so at each day's close you have an unbelievable list of unexpected blessings. Say thank you to someone you don't need to, leave an extra-generous tip ... you can create an environment of gratefulness that will surround you and change the climate you circulate in. Trust me, practice this kind of action and before you know it you'll realize that mysteriously, instead of a default mode of grumbling, you'll be living with the joy of a Rottweiler on the end of your leash.

Stop The Clock

This chapter comes with a natural challenge attached to it:

1. *For one day make a conscious effort to find something to be grateful for each and every time you feel a complaint bubbling up inside you. Yes, you'll need to be very creative and very committed to accomplish this task.*

2. *At the end of the day, intentionally journal how you feel. Did you feel better about this day than you do about those days where you give your complaints free reign?*

3. *During the next coffee or meal you share with a friend, talk about your experience and challenge them to try it for a day. You may be surprised to discover that gratitude is contagious.*

4. *Budget $10.00 to give your paper carrier or minimum wage server an extra generous tip. Watch their face light up. Watch yours too.*

CHAPTER NINE

Spirituality: Daring To Feed Your Soul

*The problem with steroids is that they produce a body
where the outside and the inside don't match.*

*If the marathon has taught me anything, it's the futility of
effort-at-the-moment-of-action-alone living.*

One of the most difficult duties I've performed as a pastor, chaplain or auxiliary policeman is described by an acronym of three letters: N.O.K. These seemingly innocuous letters stand for "Next of Kin," a phrase police use to describe the feared task of informing people that one of their loved ones has died. As you can imagine, having the police involved in such notifications typically occurs only when the death was sudden and unexpected.

My experience with N.O.K.'s has convinced me that when life comes crashing down, as it does in such moments, there is nothing an individual can do to suddenly build their soul. You either have a deep reservoir that has been built and filled in months and years prior, or you don't. There are no emergency measures one can enact in a moment of crisis to produce a well-nourished soul.

I beg not to be misunderstood. I am not saying that a healthy soul makes life's catastrophe's easy. Of course not! A catastrophe hits us all with full force, regardless the state of our soul. However, when life does crash, there is no substitute for a soul that's been well-nourished in faith and the love and hope of God.

I'm convinced the reason more people don't engage in soul care is because it doesn't show. We live in a society obsessed with appearance. I've heard it said, "One doesn't need to be well read as long as you surround yourself with books. One need not play the piano as long as you own a grand." Thank God, attitudes like those are beginning to change. Increasingly we have had our fill of "appearances" and are longing for substance. The old motto, "Fake it if you can't make it," rings hollow. We don't want to fake it. We long for what's real. When the light is turned out at night and you lay there alone, no matter who's beside you … when it's just you and God in one of those rare moments when you both look deep into your soul, there's no faking. You need to know who you are at the deepest level.

Laws Of Soul Care

It sounds arrogant to speak about LAWS of the soul but let me put it this way. If Bill Gates offered a few laws about making money, who wouldn't sit up and pay attention? If Sidney Crosby spoke about the laws of hockey or Ichiro about baseball, who wouldn't lace up? Let the reasoning continue. If the Bible, the book of God's truth provides some laws of soul care, should we not, for our own good, pay very close attention?

Law #1: Make Sure Your Soul Is Alive

Before you worry about feeding it, make sure your soul is alive.

I am going to use a Bible term, one that's been very badly abused so you're going to have to pretend you've never heard it before. Ignore all the baggage contained in this term and hear it just as the Bible uses it. Agreed?

One day Jesus was teaching about life and the Kingdom of God, teaching about soul stuff when a prominent religious leader by the name of Nicodemus came to him with a few comments and questions. In response to his comments Jesus said this (are you ready here comes the term), *"Very truly I tell you, no one can see the kingdom of God without being born again.* (John 3:3) Remember you agreed to pretend you've never heard the term before. Forget all the hoopla about the "born again" movement. I think Jesus would be embarrassed by a lot of what's gone on there too so put it right out of your mind and ask yourself instead, "What does that mean?" Nicodemus didn't understand either so he asked a few questions which resulted in Jesus explaining exactly what He meant. He was talking about spiritual birth. He was talking about becoming spiritually alive. Just as you've experienced physical birth, Jesus says, you also need to experience a spiritual birth. Nicodemus still didn't get it and continued to ask questions which led to the most famous Bible verse ever penned, John 3:16 *"For God so loved the world that he gave his one and only Son, that whoever believes in him shall not perish but have eternal life.* In other words, a spiritual birth has its roots in the love of God so extreme that His

Son died on the cross to enable us to receive it. Our response to that depth of love and grace, our acceptance of God's offer of forgiveness, our embracing God's full involvement in our life, present and future, is so contrary to our do-it-myself mindset it can rightly be described as being born all over again!

Having a soul that is alive and tender and submissive to God's touch is readily the most important ingredient to a meaningful life. That's why it's Law #1.

Law #2: Every Living Thing Requires Nurture

If your soul is alive, you've got to feed it. Spiritual birth is no more the end goal than is physical birth. As soon as something is alive it requires nourishment, and what you feed it matters. St. Paul put it this way, *"Do not be deceived: God cannot be mocked. People reap what they sow (Galatians 6:7a)."* It's called the law of the harvest. You receive out of your soul exactly what you plant in it. Why the warning? Because, as surprising as it sounds, in every era of history people have been fooled. It's mind-boggling. There is no farmer or orchardist who would dispute this law. You don't plant peas and harvest potatoes. You don't plant an apple tree and expect peaches. Yet in the moral sphere, in the soul sphere, we somehow think it's different. So we feed ourselves a steady diet of television and movies and escapist entertainment; we fill our lives with the pursuit of money and power and sexual conquest; we know the batting averages and handicaps of ball players and golfers alike; we can tell one designer label from another at fifty yards. And then we're surprised and shocked that we have empty, barren souls. Of course we do – if we haven't planted anything in them. It's a law that cannot be violated without peril.

I ride a motorcycle and almost every day someone comments about how clean it is. I mean no offense by this but that's a really dumb question. I've lost track of the hundreds of times someone has said to me, "How do you keep your bike so clean?" How do you think? *I wash it.* Do they really think God performs a little miracle that allows everyone else's vehicle to get dirty while mine stays clean? Of course not! There is no mystery. If you want a clean vehicle, wash it. If you want a well-nourished soul, feed it.

- Feed it through worship and song.

- Feed it through solitude. Just shut the noise off and meditate.

- Feed it through enriching relationships.

- Feed it by stopping the flow of junk food that normally pours in, so it develops an appetite for healthy nourishment.

- Feed it by intentional thought. Philippians 4:8 says, *"Finally, brothers and sisters, whatever is true, whatever is noble, whatever is right, whatever is pure, whatever is lovely, whatever is admirable – if anything is excellent or praiseworthy – think about such things."*

  Why? Because such thoughts nourish your soul!

Law #3: Only You Can Feed Your Soul

As I write this chapter, a prominent sports celebrity has just died. He crashed his car into the back of a tow truck on a major US freeway. At the time of the crash, he was impaired, he was speeding, he was talking on his cell phone and he wasn't wearing his seat belt. There were also drugs found in his vehicle. AND, his dad has just declared he is suing the tow company, the tow truck driver and the motorist who was being helped because he feels they are responsible for his son's death.

Unfortunately, the tragedy of the situation hides the fact that the father's attitude is unbelievably common. It's a reflection of our way of life. There is always someone else to blame, someone else responsible for the negative impacts in our life. That's why I feel compelled to point out that nourishing your soul – is *your* job. The government is not responsible for your soul and neither is the church, the school or your parents. This is one job only you can accomplish.

Stop The Clock

It's time for personal reflection. How effective are you at feeding your soul? Consider the following questions:

1. *How long has it been since you were moved by the words or power of a song? If it's been too long, chances are you are living at a pace that doesn't allow nourishment to reach deep into your soul.*

2. *How long has it been since you stole away to a quiet place and remained quiet long enough to hear the Creator whisper your name?*

3. *When did you last leave a gathering of friends feeling uplifted and encouraged? Is there anything you need to change in those gatherings?*

4. *When did you last go one day without eating spiritual junk food?*

Remember, change happens one decision at a time; it's your move ...

CHAPTER TEN
Health: You Do Have A Choice

" ... I am fearfully and wonderfully made." (Psalm 139:14)

I live in the Okanagan Valley of the interior of British Columbia, Canada. I know I am biased but any objective observer would quickly agree that this is one of the most beautiful places on earth. The mountains surround a pristine lake which itself provides water for lush orchards. It's difficult to avoid using terms like paradise when describing our valley.

While writing this chapter, we are experiencing the full-moon phase of the lunar cycle. Each evening for the past three, I have watched, speechless, as the moon has crept over the mountain top, its size and color beyond description. Its beauty has been the topic of discussion all around our little city. Additionally, I've spent the last few nights at the baseball park, watching our son play ball. High on a light standard above the park is an osprey nest. Each night we watch as the osprey parents go fishing in the lake, return with a good-sized fish tightly clasped in their talons to feed their young. It too is a sight that defies description.

Often we look at sunsets and mountains, lakes and rivers, animals, flowers and fruit trees and marvel at their beauty—and it's right that we do. Yet somewhere along the way we've lost our fascination with the part of God's creation that crowns it all: the human body.

If printing this chapter in red or insisting you read it naked in front of a mirror would underscore its importance and spur you to action, I'd do it. But I suspect all I can really do is beg. Please, please, please invest in the one and only body the Creator has given you. Invest in it every single hour. Its health and fitness impacts absolutely everything else in your life.

Barriers To Caring For Your Body

I believe so strongly in the value of physical investment I'm going to take time to first of all diffuse your arguments.

Objection #1: You Dislike People Like Me

The simple fact that you've already read several times that I am a marathon runner may have turned you off. If you haven't skipped this chapter you are most likely rolling your eyes thinking to yourself, "Oh sure, he's the marathon guy, he's just on his pet project in which he can be self-righteous." Even though you don't know me, you know people like me and they turn you off. Right? So let's deal with that first.

Taking care of YOUR body has absolutely nothing to do with me or with the fact that I run marathons. That simply happens to be my hobby. I have no more interest in turning you into a runner than I do in insisting that you ride a motorcycle, which I also do. This isn't about me, it's about YOU! One of the most foolish decisions you could make would be to avoid doing what you need to do because you don't like the way someone else does it. YOU need to take care of YOUR body regardless what I do with mine.

Objection #2: I Can't Change My Genes

No you can't. You may have some pre-disposed health issues. You definitely have a body type you inherited. You will have some genetic strengths and weaknesses that you can't change, only manage. So, it's critical that you understand that we are not talking about putting you on the cover of a health and fitness magazine. We're not talking about anyone else's artificial definition of what your body ought to look like. What we are talking about is being the best steward possible of the body God gave you. That principle applies whether your entire family history screams "cancer," if you're confined to a wheelchair or if you're an Olympic athlete.

Objection #3: I'd Sooner Worry About My Soul Than My Body

Good for you, but who says it has to be either/or. Besides, it was God who provided your soul with a place to live. Furthermore, the Scriptures suggest your body is also a place for God to live. "Do you not know that your body is a temple of the Holy Spirit, who is in you, whom you have received from God (1 Cor. 6:19)." And then get this, St. Paul, who seemed to have some body image issues himself says in the next verse , "You are not your own; you were bought at a price. Therefore honor God WITH YOUR BODIES." The distinction we've made for years about God only being concerned about our soul or spirit is clearly contrary to the teaching of the Bible. God is vitally concerned about the whole person, including the assembly of cells and bones and muscles and organs He created.

So, let me summarize. Investing in your health has nothing to do with me or any other fitness freak. It has to do with helping you be the healthiest you can be, regardless of your limitations, in direct response to God's expectation of you.

Why Should You Take Fitness Seriously?

1. Do It For God

The case for fitness has already been established so I'll make this quick, but, if you claim to be a follower of God you cannot ignore your body. Consider these questions while thinking about your health and fitness.

a. Who Made You?

This is not a trick question. It's an issue that must be faced. Genesis 2:7 declares that the Lord God Himself formed us. We are His special creation. It only stands to reason that we are responsible and answerable to our Creator for the manner in which we treat His creation.

b. Who Lives In You?

Recently several provinces in Canada have passed laws banning smoking in vehicles if there is a child under the age of 16 inside. A recent interview with smokers revealed that almost all of them agree with the law. Imagine that, they agree that if a child is inside, they must refrain from behaviour that would be harmful.

If you're a Christian, God is inside. Will you dare defile Him?

I'm teeing off on this point because I've had long lines of Christians argue that fitness is not a spiritual matter. Think again, the conclusion is unavoidable.

2. Do It For Your Loved Ones

This may be one of the most controversial points I'll make in this day of individual rights and privileges. In every area of life from wearing seat belts to abortion people declare, "It's MY body, I'll do with it as I please." What utter nonsense! Of course what you do with your body impacts you, but it also impacts everyone who loves you.

I want to apply a Bible verse in a way we usually don't. I've thought it through carefully and am convinced the principles are sound.

1 Timothy 5:8 is a tough verse, dealing primarily with hard work and physical support of one's family. Here's what it says: *"Anyone who does not provide for their relatives, and especially for their own household, has denied the faith and is worse than an unbeliever."* (Some translations use the word "infidel")

Principle: If you don't take care of preventable (and that's a key word) health issues to the extent that they interfere with your ability to care for your family, this verse applies to you. You owe it to your loved ones, to your spouse, to your children and grandchildren to be as healthy as you possibly can be. It is God's order of things.

3. Do It For Yourself

This is so well documented I hate to repeat the obvious. Exercise alone, proper exercise, increases energy levels, elevates metabolic rates, improves blood circulation, strengthens muscles, strengthens bones, decreases blood pressure, decreases stress, develops aerobic capacity, improves sleep patterns and heightens sexual drive.

Why would anybody not want that? Especially the last one?

So, invest in your body, for God, for your loved ones and for yourself.

Now, let's talk about HOW.

Dealing With The How Of Fitness

Honestly, are you expecting any surprises here? I didn't think so. This is about THE most highly documented topic in North America today. But I'm going to keep preaching it until it sinks in. Here are 5 non-surprising suggestions about how you can invest in your health. Start this hour and stay at it every hour.

1. Be Purposeful In What You Put Into Your Body

A while back a friend of mine loaned me a 25-year-old cookbook specializing in simple, balanced, healthy diets. Let me give you one quote: *"God's people wander in the supermarket among chemical frozen pies, over-processed skillet dinners, nutrition-less snack food and soft drinks in throw-away bottles."(source unknown)*

It's like wandering through a mine-field just waiting for the explosion. Many of you have the good habit of saying grace before you eat. Right? I hope you do. Let me give you a challenge.

For the next thirty days every time you say grace, ask yourself this question: Do I have any business asking God to bless what I'm about to put in my body. A typical grace includes the phrase, "Bless this food to our bodies use." Friends, there are some things even God can't do.

Our diets have put us on a crash course with a health crisis. It's just that simple. What you put into your body, hour by hour, day by day is one of the greatest determiners of your health and fitness. Open any newspaper or magazine and you'll read statistics declaring that 60% of North Americans are overweight. 25% are officially obese. For men that means we carry more than 25% body fat and women, more than 30%. I know and you know that the reasons people overeat are complex, but for God's sake and yours, they MUST be faced and overcome.

Perhaps the most bothersome corollary to this disaster is that it's not just adults. We are continually being confronted by the fact that we are raising a generation of unhealthy children. Obesity is rapidly becoming the health crisis of the next generation. And it is fully preventable. Schools are opening their cafeterias to fast-food franchises and pop machines. If you were on a mission to make today's child as unhealthy as possible it would be impossible to devise a better plan.

I first woke up to this fact more than a dozen ago when we got a puppy. We went to the pet store where I listened for fifteen minutes to a staff member explain the nutritional benefits of each kind of dog food and how important it was to make sure we were feeding our new puppy correctly. I bought the best food on the market and then we jumped in the van and went to a fast food outlet for a cholesterol burger and heart attack fries. That's when it hit me, something wasn't adding up. You don't have to be extreme, just wise and balanced in your diet. And do it every hour.

2. *Exercise, Exercise, Exercise*

Since I've already made the case for this, let me offer a few tips on "how to" engage in the essential discipline of exercise. This is especially important since most of us have made attempts in this area before, and failed.

The single most important factor in exercise is to find a form of it you enjoy. You see, the key aspect of exercise is sustainability and you will never sustain something you don't like. Make it fun. Don't be overwhelmed by magazine articles that put down one form of exercise because some other form burns slightly more calories. You won't burn any calories, no matter how great the exercise, if you don't do it, and you won't if you don't like it.

Second, find someone to exercise with you. Even the most disciplined individuals will have days when you just don't feel like doing it. It's those times when an exercise partner or two are worth their weight in gold. Besides, if exercise takes on a social component for you, you are miles ahead of the game. Think about it, what do most of our social encounters involve? Food! Unhealthy food at that! So if you develop a social circle that engages in exercise, it's a double win.

Third, set attainable goals. Goals keep you accountable. I've found it very beneficial in my physical goal setting to focus more on the activity than the results. It's much more manageable to say I'll drink four glasses of water before lunch time and walk for 15 minutes each noon hour than it is to say I'll lose five pounds. Drink the water and take the steps, sooner or later you'll lose the weight.

Fourth, realize that a little bit of exercise is better than no exercise. I'll devote an entire chapter to the "all-or nothing" mindset, but no where does it apply more directly than in caring for yourself physically. So what if you can't get the desired amount of exercise in. Do what you can, even fifteen minutes is better than no minutes.

Have you captured what has just been said? Do something you like, with people you like, on a regular basis, and do even a bit of it if you can't do it all. Doesn't that sound better than saying, "I've got to get into a disciplined exercise regiment?" If it doesn't sound too bad, then please, please, please, do it.

3. Put Some Margin In Your Life

Dr. Richard Svenson wrote a whole book on this, simply titled, Margins. You know what margins are, the white edge around the page where there is no writing. In fact there's no anything; just blank space. We all need blank space. A leading contributor to health concerns is stress. Most of us live faster and harder without breaks than we ever dreamed we would. The Creator designed our bodies to need a day off every seven. He designed our bodies to need a good night's sleep, every night He designed us to need a mix of good hard work followed by rest, recreation and relaxation; you can't fool His plan for long.

4. Repair and Maintenance

In the last two months I've had a colonoscopy and some major dental work. If you don't know what a colonoscopy is, tonight when you get down on your knees to say your prayers, thank God. The reason I tell you these rather personal details is because the truth is, health maintenance is not all fun and games. It's inconvenient at best. But it is an essential part of taking care of ourselves.

This very moment as you read this page, you may have a heart condition or pre-cancerous polyps or who knows what else going on in your body, and you don't even know it. And you won't know it until it's too late unless you get in a routine of repair and maintenance. If you need to, set this book down right now and call your doctor for a check-up.

5. Avoid Quacks, Fads and Extremes

Just avoid them. I would be willing to bet right now that a scary number of you are reading this chapter believing that some extreme diet is going to change your life in three weeks. I guarantee you it won't. There is no shortcut to wellness. The key to any health plan is sustainability: it must become a life style. Nobody is going to eat cabbage soup the rest of their life. You know that. So, the next time you read about, or some well meaning friend tells you about a plan that's just too good to be true, just smile to yourself, nod and remember, you know better!

Whose Responsibility Is It?

Who is responsible for your health? Any guesses? I assume you've heard the old spiritual that says, "Not my brother not my sister but it's me O Lord ..." That's the answer. Your health care is not your doctor's responsibility. It's not your dentist's. It's not your spouse's. You and you alone will stand before God and give account for how you treated the very pinnacle of His creation.

It's ironic that in this day where there's such a fascination with the human body, very little of it has translated into wise, daily, hourly action. So once again, I plead with you, please, please, please invest in your health.

Stop The Clock

Motivation is so important. We can have full intention to live a healthy lifestyle but if we lack motivation, our plans quickly slip away.

1. *What is YOUR motivation to adopt a healthier lifestyle?*

2. *Who will help you make wise choices minute by minute, hour by hour, day by day?*

It is a daunting challenge to attempt to live a healthy lifestyle in an unhealthy household. Adopt some family goals that will get everyone on the right path.

PART THREE

COMMON INVESTMENT PITFALLS

CHAPTER ELEVEN
ALL OR NOTHING:
THE PARALYSIS OF PERFECTION

Rare is the person who, if they can't vacuum
the whole house, vacuums one room

You've been given some VERY dangerous advice. It may have never appeared to you as dangerous because in part, it is great advice. But, it is very, very dangerous! Here it is: *"Always finish what you start."*

Hold it in that part of your brain where you hold things and let me tell you a story that, on the surface appears to have nothing to do with the advice we just discussed.

One spring not too long ago I went to a rental shop to rent a lawn thatcher. It immediately became evident that the proprietor knew I was the local Baptist preacher. It was also evident that he had not frequented church in quite some time. I can always spot those individuals because they try to appear religious, but don't quite make it. In his case the give away was that he called me Reverend as if it was my first name. "Oh Reverend," he said, "You bet we have lawn thatchers. In fact we just got a brand new shipment of Honda's. Come on back and I'll show you how they work." I was reasonably sure I knew how it worked but he clearly wanted to give me a demonstration.

"Reverend," he said, "these new thatchers are the cat's meow. They start first time every time." With that, he flipped a few switches and gave a mighty pull on the rope. The thatcher didn't start. With a furrow of perplexity on his brow he said, "That's funny, it always starts." He gave another pull. Not even a sputter. He adjusted a few things and pulled again. Nothing. This time, however, he swore. Then, remembering I was standing right behind him, he apologized, "Sorry, Reverend," he said. After that he got into a bit of a routine. He pulled, he swore, he apologized. Pulled, swore, apologized, it was hilarious.

While all that was going on, and the perspiration running down his forehead, I took a closer look at the thatcher. It was a Honda. I've ridden motorcycles most of my life, several of them Honda's, so I immediately noticed something that should have been obvious to him, but wasn't. Like most motorbikes, the thatcher had a Start or Run switch that needed to be in the "on" position for it to start. This one was securely in the position marked "off." He could have tugged on that rope all day long, but as long as the "start" switch remained "off" there would be no action. Thinking there could be some humor in the moment, I offered to take a turn at the rope. He gave me a look that could only be interpreted to mean, "If I can't get it going, what the *&^% is a 'reverend' going to do?" So he rejected my offer to help and kept on pulling, and swearing, and apologizing. He checked the carburetor, he checked the plugs and he pulled some more. Finally, after he was completely worn out, I again offered to take a turn. Reluctantly he agreed. With his gaze momentarily fixed in the other direction I flipped the switch to "Start," leaned down, gave one effortless tug and watched as the thatcher roared to life. You could have knocked him over with a feather. I couldn't resist saying to him, "Don't worry buddy, it was a miracle."

In that moment, and in many moments since when that experience has come to mind, I've remembered the one truth it exposes. No matter how good something appears, no matter how grandiose the dream, no matter how great the plan, no matter how solid the intentions, it is all useless until the "start" switch gets pressed. A great plan is just that, a great plan, until you actually begin working it.

Now, re-activate that dangerous piece of advice you put on hold from the begin-

> *...it is all useless until the "start" switch gets pressed.*

ning of the chapter. Remember it? "*Always finish what you start.*" What great advice! I gave it to my kids. I taught them from their earliest years, "Schroeders aren't quitters. We finish what we start, even if it's tough." So what's wrong with that incredible advice? Nothing, UNLESS, you are so obsessed with finishing that it keeps you from ever starting.

We've all heard motivational speakers ask us to identify how many unfinished projects we have laying around the basement. How many things we've started but never completed. They have a point. But, my point is this, how many more projects have we never even started. How many projects exist only in our dreams?

How often have we planned and planned and planned, then worked on perfecting the plan some more, and then never done anything with them? They've remained just that, plans! We've been so consumed with perfect plans, perfect executions and perfect finishes, we've never pressed the start button.

The principle of Life By The Hour faces the reality that some hours all you can do is make a beginning. Some days, all you can accomplish is one more little step; BUT, it is one more step. Failure to understand that life is a step by step, hour by hour journey rather than a gigantic, instantaneous accomplishment has kept many from taking any steps, and has caused even more to take unsustainable steps.

If you think this principle overstates reality let your mind roam to the number of times you or someone you love fits the following scenarios.

- Unable to commit to lose 25 lbs until after Christmas, we lose 0 lbs. Or, worse yet, we use it as rationalization to gain 5 lbs.

- Unable to save $300 per month (or whatever is a meaningful amount for you) until after the car is paid off, we save nothing.

- Unable to write the entire term paper (or sermon) we write nothing.

The t-shirt that proclaims "Go Big Or Go Home," has, unfortunately caused many to go home. They have never realized the joy or victory of a small step.

The entire premise of this book is that God designed life to be lived one step at a time, *the most important step of all being the first one.*

Rare indeed is the person, who, if they can't vacuum the whole house, vacuums one room. Those who do possess an amazing secret!

Stop The Clock

Think of something you would like to accomplish; something meaningful, purposeful and important – but you haven't started to work on it yet.

1. *Is it possible that "an all or nothing attitude" is what is holding you back?*

2. *Is there a small step you could take today that would get you started?*

3. *How will you celebrate beginning your project?*

4. *Get out your calendar. Mark down small steps you know you can accomplish each day for the next 14 days. Resist the temptation to attempt too much.*

CHAPTER TWELVE
DANGEROUS DISTRACTIONS

As I watched him drive into the car in front of him. I wondered,
"How will he explain this one to his wife?"

I have a favorite restaurant. It's located on the second floor overlooking beautiful Lake Okanagan. One summer day while having lunch in that location, a steady stream of bikini-clad beauties strolled through the park across the street. I didn't notice them of course, but was told they were there. What I did notice was a man driving down the street so engrossed by the beautiful young ladies he failed to notice the car in front of him had stopped. The collision could be heard for blocks. As I watched him crash into the car in front of him, I wondered, "How will he explain this one to his wife?"

How long has it been since distractions have interrupted your plans and intentions? An hour? Half an hour? Five minutes?

Perhaps the second most common investment pitfall, next to not taking the critical first step, is to allow ourselves to be quickly distracted. To be sure, the distractions are usually by a bevy of good ideas, but they are distractions nevertheless and focus is gone.

A lot of people, for many varying reasons, miss the best God has in store for them. I don't want to be one of those people.

Recently I sat at a table in a quiet beachfront park. I read and re-read a couple favorite texts from the Gospel of Luke. The first one described Jesus' incomparable ability to focus (Luke 5:15-16). Reading those verses one gets the impression a nuclear bomb could have gone off beside Him and He would still focus on showing compassion to people and spending time with His Heavenly Father. The second text I read described me, and I suspect, you. It's the story of people who were so busy and so distracted with the duties of life that they kept missing things of ultimate value (Luke 14:15-24).

Sitting in the park reading and re-reading those two texts, I wrote these words:

A lot of people, for many varying reasons, miss the best God has in store for them. I don't want to be one of those people.

I don't. Do you? What will keep it from happening?

One of my heroes, who has had so much influence on me is pastor and author John Ortberg. I exaggerate only slightly by saying that John has made a career of fighting against one word. Without question he has convinced me of its danger and I've gotten to the point where I'll nominate it as the single biggest enemy to a meaningful life. I admit it is easily the biggest enemy to my soul. The one word is, "Hurry."

At the root of "hurry" is the belief that if I do life faster, I can jam more into it. But is that what I really need, more squeezed into my life? Hurry is epidemic. I was recently in a drive through line-up at Canada's famous coffee spot, Tim Horton's, and noticed you can now purchase Speed Passes. Now even getting coffee and do-nuts doesn't need to consume so much of your life. Faster, faster. I read on-line of a new term in use, it's the "honka-second." That's the amount of time it takes from the moment the light turns green until the first horn sounds. Faster, faster.

A while back one of the local radio stations was on location at one of those speed monitoring centers. It was an encouragement for everyone to slow down. I had my radio tuned to their station and as I went through the DJ recognized me and said, on the air, "That was Pastor Tim Schroeder who just zoomed by us … he's the faster pastor." Subsequently, everywhere I went for weeks people called me the faster pastor. I sort of smiled inside, think-ing, yeah, that's me alright, busy, hurrying about God's work. The problem is, I don't know of one single, hurting individual who longs for a faster pastor.

I'm not trying to make a federal case of this, there are other enemies to a flourishing life, but for me, I nominate hurry as en-emy #1. In all our hurry we only scratch the surface of the depth God planned for us to enjoy. Life is a constant distraction in every direction.

Carl Jung, father of analytical psychology once wrote, "Hurry is not of the devil; hurry is the devil." Theologically I may strug-gle with the totality of his statement, practically; it contains a lot of truth.

How can I keep my life from the curse of hurry and distraction?

Face The Shallowness Of My Excuses

Everyone is busy. Everyone! The question is whether I'll let busy-ness rob me of what I both want and need. The Bible text I referenced at the beginning of this chapter got so deeply under my skin because it declared that everyone missed out on the special banquet being offered because they ALL made excuses. That's a dead give away. What is the likelihood that they ALL had good reasons not to attend the banquet? It gets worse when you read the story and discover the reasons they gave were ludicrous. One said, I've just bought a field and must go see it. Another said he'd just bought some oxen and needed to test drive them. At least the third guy had an excuse that rings true. He said he'd just gotten married and his wife wouldn't let him go. Actually that's not quite true. In those days wives had no say. The whole point is that they ALL missed the banquet, which represented the kingdom of God, for the dumbest of reasons.

Have times changed? Have they changed for me? If I'm going to win this battle I need to face the shallowness of my excuses.

Expose The Dark Side Of My Motives

Refusing to be caught up in hurry and distraction involves facing and admitting why I like the distraction. Jesus, Who arguably had a busier schedule than mine, always found time to withdraw to lonely places to pray. Why don't I?

Wrestling with that question did indeed expose some dark motives. Is it because I like to be popular? I like to be liked? I'm afraid that if I withdraw to pray, I might miss something? If I'm not in the crowds will people forget me? The truth is that I've become so used to being busy and distracted that it forms part of my identity. Stepping back from the rush is a risk. But, if I don't, I might find myself missing the real banquet of life for some pretty stupid reasons.

Accept Responsibility For My Own Choices

Ask almost anyone why they're too busy and they'll tell you. And it will always be someone else's fault. My boss, my family, my church, my this, my that, REQUIRE me to do it all. Which begs the question, who's life is it anyway?

The point of the story of the missed banquet is ironically often missed itself. We get so caught up discussing the reasons *why* people missed the dinner that we forget – *they missed the dinner!* They missed it. And the bottom line is, it doesn't matter why, if you miss it, you miss it and no one else is responsible.

I love to emphasize forgiveness. In my opinion it's one of the greatest truths in the world. However, forgiveness never promises to return one moment to you. That moment is gone. What we stand in desperate need of is a ruthlessness in acknowledging that we are responsible for every moment of our life to the point that we, not our boss, not our society, not even our church, will make those decisions.

Stop The Clock

The next time you enjoy a few moments of solitude ask yourself:

1. *What precious opportunity have I missed lately for which I blamed someone else?*

2. *What types of distractions are most dangerous to me? Is it popularity, money, sexual conquest, trying to appear successful? What have I been trading for them that I refuse to trade any longer?*

3. *Right now, this hour, am I doing what I'd be doing if I knew I had 30 days to live?*

CHAPTER THIRTEEN
VEGGING IS NOT AN INVESTMENT

"Go to the ant, you sluggard;
consider its ways and be wise!" (Proverbs 6:6)

"A little sleep, a little slumber,
a little folding of the hands to rest – and poverty will come on you
like a thief and scarcity like an armed man." (Proverbs 6:10-11)

You are not going to like this chapter! I don't like this chapter, but unfortunately it's necessary. I am going to expose one of the biggest investment myths of our day. It's likely you nodded in affirmation at the description of a hurried, harried life in the previous chapter. It's even more likely that you agree that our stress-filled pace of life is an enemy that must be overcome. The myth isn't found in the diagnosis. The diagnosis is bang on. The myth is found in the most frequently prescribed cure. The myth is that the solution to an over-paced, stress-filled life is to do nothing.

Think real hard, how many people do you know for whom stress leave has worked? Maybe you have no experience with stress leave, so try this one. After a very stressful, busy day, which evening activity leaves you more refreshed: sitting in front of the television for three hours or going for a walk with your spouse or a good friend followed by an hour and a half working on a hobby?

Vegging is not an investment. Vegging doesn't work. We weren't created to veg. We were created to create and produce and recreate and fellowship and worship. The stress-filled life is not typically a result of over-work; it's most often the result of unproductive work, of spinning our wheels, of seeing no reward for our labor. The solution is not to cease activity and become as much like a form of plant life as possible, the solution is to find rewarding and productive activity.

The myth is that the solution to an over-paced, stress-filled life is to do nothing.

In their book, Made To Count, Bob Record and Randy Singer state that deep down inside, one of the greatest fears we ALL possess is to come to the end of our lives without having made a significant difference. Yes! So why do so many shout, "TGIF?" Why is the stated goal of so many to make enough money as quickly as possible so they can lie on a beach and do nothing? We contradict our inner most nature. Nothing else explains why Rick Warren's Purpose Driven Life sold multiple millions of copies. Nothing else explains why Abraham Maslow's "Hierarchy of Needs," studied by every psychology student in the last fifty years has at the apex of the hierarchy: *self-actualization*. It seems that when the Creator put His thumbprint on human life, part of that imprint was a compelling need for each and every one of us to fulfill a Divine purpose. Vegging, appealing as it is some days, contradicts our very raison d'etre.

The Alternative

The alternative to this investment pitfall is to remind yourself as often as necessary of three affirming truths. Repeat them hourly if you need to, until they become your default mode of thinking replacing the urge to veg.

Truth #1: God Knows Exactly What I Need Right Now.

The Gospel writers all pen some version of this assurance. Matthew writes, "Are not two sparrows sold for a penny? Yet not one of them will fall to the ground apart from the will of your Father. And even the very hairs of your head are all numbered. So don't be afraid; you are worth more than many sparrows (Matt. 10:29-31). God is intimately acquainted with you and knows precisely what you need to get through the next hour and the next ten years.

He knows your name. Telephone solicitors try to copy this level of intimacy, often with disastrous pronunciation results. I've answered the phone and heard, "Hi, is this Mr. Scroter?" Worse yet is when they don't understand that I use the initial of my first name but go by my second name. So they ask for, "Mr. PTim Scroter." I know immediately who I have on the other end of the line. God doesn't fake it. Jesus compares Himself to the Good

Shepherd and says that His sheep know and listen to His voice and He calls them by name.

He knows your vocation and interests. Read the Bible some time through "occupational lenses." You'll read about Amos the shepherd, Cain the farmer, Deborah the judge, Luke the physician, Matt the tax man, Lydia the fabric dealer, Peter and Andrew the fishermen. From shepherds to farmers to soldiers to business women, to slaves, God shows interest in the real details and pressures of our lives.

If you are about to crash and burn and the thought of the next hour is overwhelming, affirm loudly and clearly, that God knows you and knows exactly what you need right now.

Truth #2: God Has Placed The Need To Produce In Me.

In the hurriedness of our day we've become convinced that all activity is bad. Some activity may be bad and too much activity may be even worse but that does not make the reverse true, that inactivity is sacred. Remember, the desire to create and produce and accomplish is God-given. The opening words of the Bible are, "In the beginning God created …" (Genesis 1:1). He then very quickly established humankind in the garden and gave them something to do. Remember, this was before the infamous fruit-salad incident. Many people assume work is our punishment for sin. Wrong. It was introduced before the fall. It's part of what fulfills us.

If you have any doubt as to the validity of this truth, just watch children. They build things, color things, draw things, sometimes for hours at a time. They bring it to you and say, "Look Mommy, look Daddy, and they swell with pride." God who made you and knows your name has also placed inside you a whole bunch of talents, abilities and gifts and has breathed into you the need to do something with them. Squelching that innate need will not help you either survive or flourish.

Truth #3: Living In My God-Given Calling Is Liberty.

You will never be more alive than when you are doing what you were created and called to do. A corollary to that is that you will never be more alive than when you are learning even more about what you were created and called to do. That's called investing.

My wife Arlene is one of the hardest workers I know. She is a gastro-intestinal nurse who works full-time. Yet it was not uncommon for her to come home after a long, stressful shift, and if our son had a group of friends over for the evening, I would hear some clanging in the kitchen. Before long the odor of freshly baked chocolate chip cookies would waft through the air. I'd say to her, "Sweetheart, sit down. Put your feet up. Relax. Veg." And she'd look right back at me and say, "I am relaxing. There's nothing I'd sooner do than take some warm cookies and cold milk downstairs for the boys." It's part of who she is created to be and she is never happier than when she's doing it.

God knows you; He has placed the need to create and produce in you; and you will never be more alive and content than when you are engaged in doing what He has created you to do.

Is there a place for rest? Of course! But I ask again, "When do you feel more rested and refreshed, after an evening in front of the television, or after an evening investing in your life?"

Stop The Clock

1. *Take a few minutes and attempt to honestly describe the kinds of activities that energize and refresh you.*

2. *When you get really busy and stressed out, which of those activities get eliminated from your schedule? Think seriously about this. Does it make any sense that at the time you need refreshment most, you eliminate the very activities that provide it?*

3. *Recruit your spouse or a close friend to help you with this. The next time you find yourself "totally beat" and are on the verge of vegging, ask them to nudge you to engage in one of your refreshing activities instead. Watch your spirit rise!*

CHAPTER FOURTEEN
INVESTMENT DRUDGERY

Variety isn't just the spice of life ...
it's a core part of the menu.

Thirty-one summers ago I was a sod harvester. From a distance it looked like the perfect job for a young, athletic male. I made great money, in fact, enough to buy an engagement ring and go back to school in the fall. I wound up in the best physical condition of my life. Body fat percentages that wouldn't have even registered had anyone bothered to test me. (Oh to be there again)! I had a deep tan, very little stress and money to spend. Like I said, it was great, from a distance. In reality, I hated every minute of it. I woke up each morning at 4:30 and rushed to the window to see if it had rained enough overnight that work would be cancelled. I couldn't wait for the summer to end. Why? Certainly not because it was too hard! I enjoy hard work. Not because it was outside, I love the out of doors. And, did I mention, the money was great? I hated it simply because it was the most boring job I've ever had. Stack sod on a pallet, get a new pallet, stack more sod on that pallet, get a new pallet, stack more sod … you get the picture. I did it hour after hour, day after day, week after week. Thirty-one years have passed and I'm sure I could still stack a perfect pallet of sod.

Monotony destroys initiative. A few years ago I mentioned publicly that my favorite Christmas song is, "Go Tell It On The Mountain." A couple weeks later I received a custom-burned CD containing eighteen different versions of it. I played it once, played it a second time and put it away. I love the song, but thirty-six times was about thirty too many.

I don't know any force more certain to keep you from making the strategic investments described in the previous section, than drudgery and monotony.

Here are several investment drudgeries certain to destroy any initiative you have to build into your life:

One Size Fits All

Every time someone tells you of a method "you must use to improve," just call "Baloney." I have simply had enough of authors of fad diets who claim they hold the only secret to weight loss. I'm tired of preachers telling me exactly what I have to do to have a healthy relationship with God. Experience has revealed that most often their secret is what they happen to be selling. I've had my fill of people who've found "success" through one method, and insist I do the same. I admire their zeal, but not their insight. Imagine the gall of people who have never met you, who don't know your personality, background, abilities or disabilities attempting to tell you how to keep growing. You need to discover what works for you.

Several years ago author Gary Thomas wrote <u>Sacred Pathways,</u> in which he destroyed the one size fits all approach to God. Acknowledging that there are clearly some absolutes given by God Himself, Gary liberated us by urging us toward the pathways that move *us* closer to God. If solitude works for you, great, but perhaps you feel closest to God in moments where you are sharing relationship. That's great too! Maybe God touches your heart when you're serving the poor. Fantastic! Maybe it's when you sing and pray. Fantastic too! Find your path and don't be bullied into someone else's.

> *You need to discover what works for you.*

Branding

Promoters of a disciplined life-style may chafe at what I'm about to say, but only momentarily. The truth is, what I'm suggesting requires even more discipline.

Resist predictability! I know, you've read that you're supposed to make good behavior a habit. Some will even tell you how many habits successful people are supposed to have. That's great. Just make sure you interrupt your habits before they become meaningless and boring ruts.

Resist predictability! Corporations world-wide seek universally recognizable branding. When you see their sign they want you to know that their hamburger or cup of coffee or pair of jeans is 100% predictable. That's fine for coffee or jeans but it'll suck the joy and inspiration out of your life. Eat the same meal, run the same route, sing the same song, make love the same way, do anything predictably day after day and you will lose interest no matter how healthy it is or how much you enjoy it.

Resist predictability! When you pray, write a letter to God one day. Get down on your knees before Him the next. Sing your prayer as a song of worship from time to time. Pray with a friend. Go for a walk with God and carry on very personal conversation.

Resist predictability! I've found as a runner who's covered thousands of kilometers that it's essential for me to rarely run the same route two days in a row. One day I'll run long, the next day short. One day I'll run on hills, the next day flat. Some days I run alone, and savor the quietness. Other days I run with a friend or with a group. Some days I don't run at all and enjoy the change.

Resist predictability!

Should

Investing in your life without question requires discipline, but is rarely encouraged through guilt. A friend said to me one day, "Tim don't should on yourself." Great advice! The challenge is to find initiatives that work for me in my particular station of life and to joyfully and creatively embrace them.

My personal weakness is to confuse the discipline with the goal. I've occasionally forgotten that my goal is health and have run myself into injury, at which point, of course, I couldn't run at all and the goal was jeopardized. Should, will do that to you.

Final Observation

Life By The Hour is a strategy for living that focuses on establishing a life pattern that makes small, valuable investments so that when the times come for withdrawal, your bank account will be strong. Learn to make those strategic investments and watch out for common investment pitfalls.

Stop The Clock

1. *It's time to break predictability. Take an inventory of your life over the past month. Do you see any ruts or routines that are becoming boring? Would your life make a great plot for a book or movie or would it be a snoozer? What can you change-up?*

2. *Think of "HOW" you can make some changes. Consider some of these variations:*

   a. *try a different form of exercise than your usual*

   b. *read a book that is unlike the genre you usually read*

   c. *drive a new route to work, even if it takes longer; better yet, ride your bike to work several days a week*

   d. *experiment with food from a different culture*

   e. *if you are over 45, spend some time talking with a teenager; if you're under 45 do the same with a senior*

   f. *get away from people and talk to God – OUT LOUD*

PART FOUR

SURVIVAL STRATEGIES

CHAPTER FIFTEEN

FORGIVENESS BY THE HOUR:
When Wrongs Threaten To Win

You are not God. You don't have the power to forgive once-for-all, so why not try it for just the next hour!

Many sincere Christians will question the above statement. That's okay, question it, real hard. There's no downside to having you think about forgiveness, even if you disagree with me.

A scene repeated in my office with greater frequency than I care to admit goes something like this. A husband and wife come in, take seats beside each other while maintaining as much space between them as possible. They sit there staring at the floor. Finally, after a few moments of strained silence, one of them, usually the husband blurts out, "I had an affair. I told her I'm sorry but she can't forgive me."

Although not at all gifted as a counselor I know enough to ask a few insightful questions and discover that his wife only found out about the affair two days earlier. I also realize that he is looking for something not likely to occur, forgiveness that is both instantaneous and absolute. He fails to comprehend an essential truth:

Forgiveness is more a process than an event.

We live in a time where the capacity to forgive has become an essential life-skill. Over time my voice mail has recorded dozens of devastating messages like these:

> *"Hey Tim, thought I'd let you know, my wife just*
> *left me, and yes, there is someone else."*

> *"Hi Pastor Tim, can we come in and see you? We just*
> *found out our 4-year-old daughter has been*
> *molested by my older brother?"*

> *"Tim, I really need to see you. I got caught stealing at*
> *work and have just been fired. I'm afraid to go home."*

> *"Pastor Tim, will you talk to my parents with me? I'm pregnant."*

Forgiveness is more a process than an event.

Do messages like these indicate that a life of meaning and joy is now out of the reach for the people involved, or is there life beyond tragedy? Like it or not, life involves pain, much of it inflicted on us by people we thought we could trust and even worse, much of it inflicted on us by ourselves. What then? How do you live when "wrongs" threaten to dominate your life? More importantly, is it possible to not just survive moments like these, but to arrive at a place where once again you can flourish?

While processing your own struggle with forgiveness, remember that no lesser a person than St. Peter came to Jesus one day asking, "How many times do I have to forgive someone who wrongs me? Seven times?" Clearly Peter was having issues with someone. I can only imagine the smile on Jesus' face when he replied, "No Peter, seventy times seven." (Matthew 18:21-22). Jesus was indicating that forgiveness is not a one time act but rather a demeanor that gets lived out hour by hour.

The Importance Of The Forgiveness Journey

Whether or not you choose to take the forgiveness journey really matters. It would be easy to provide a long list of reasons but I'll restrain myself to just a few.

First, forgiveness right-sizes the wrong that was committed. We don't like to admit it but most of us exaggerate and sensationalize our hurts. The moment you choose to walk the road of forgiveness you are forced to be gut-wrenchingly honest about what happened, without either minimizing it or making it grandiose. In every case forgiveness involves confronting the wrong which requires facing the truth about what actually took place. (*I strongly suggest you stop and re-read this paragraph*).

Second, forgiveness encourages authenticity. Forgiveness is a rare commodity because many of us prefer not to admit things aren't perfect in our life. To forgive means to come out from hiding and address the issues in our lives and families and work places. Cover-ups get exposed and reality gets a chance.

Third, forgiveness is a matter of importance because failure to deal with issues allows the unresolved junk to actually become the defining feature of your life. Without ten seconds of thought you could list a number of people who are defined by their bitterness. You hear their name and the wrong perpetrated against them immediately surfaces. If you met them you wouldn't think of asking how they are because they'd tell you and it wouldn't be pretty. My question is, "Do you really want to be one of them?"

Fourth, forgiveness matters because it frees you to live in the present and dream about the future. In one of his letters St. Paul says that a key ingredient to help one move forward is a healthy sense of forgetfulness. It's impossible to go very far in life before you accumulate some baggage. Perhaps you were abused as a youngster, your parents split at a strategic stage of your life, alcoholism runs in your family, you got pregnant as a teenager, were involved in substance abuse, had a marriage or two that didn't work, a career path that definitely did not go up the ladder, are plagued by secret sins that have eaten away at your self-confidence causing you to live in terror that you'll be found out. The simple fact is that as life goes on, we all accumulate quite a list of sin and failure and hurt and pain. All of us! Some of it is sin done to us and some of it our own contribution. One doesn't need to be much of a therapist to realize that if you keep picking this stuff up and never set any of it down, permanently, pretty soon your load becomes so heavy that going on is out of the question. Forgiveness allows you to get free of the junk so you can live and dream again.

Why Is It So Hard?

If forgiveness is so vital, why is it so hard? Forgiveness has eluded many of us because of the preponderance of faulty thinking that surrounds it.

Flaw number one is that many fail to account for the costly nature of forgiveness. They tritely quote the Lord's Prayer which says we should forgive others as God has forgiven us. What they forget is that God's forgiveness cost the death of Jesus Christ on the cross. Forgiveness has never been a simple event, not even for God. In every case it is costly and complex.

Flaw number two is that many assume forgiveness is about the "other person." I'm often asked, "Do I need to forgive someone who isn't sorry for what they've done?" My answer is, "Who is forgiveness about, them or you?" Forgiveness is your response to a wrong and is not dependent on the wrong doer. Of course it makes it easier when the offender is repentant, but that's their part not yours.

Flaw number three is that we fail to recognize the process nature of forgiveness. There is a marked difference between letting go of the hurt and pain, and rebuilding the trust. Men especially have an amazing ability to compartmentalize life and fail to realize that trust is not magically regained with the uttering of the two simple words, "I'm sorry." Trust is regained hour by hour.

Flaw number four involves the present day era of "human rights." When you dig all the way down to the core, you discover that forgiveness involves surrendering your right to be hurt. You choose the higher value of healing and give up the right to focus on your sense of violation.

The final flaw in thinking has to do with the challenge most of us have in forgiving ourselves. It is always amazing that those who seem so willing to forgive others are so hard on themselves when they mess up. I suspect it stems from a faulty view of God. We assume God feels about us the way we feel about ourselves and fail to take into account that in all His holiness and justice, He is also, in His very nature, "Love." He is all about restoration, as costly as it is. A solid understanding that God is for us not against us, enables us to move beyond the self-condemning attitude that makes forgiveness just beyond our grasp.

Forgiveness By The Hour

In essence, what I'm saying in this chapter is that the ability to forgive, both others and yourself is an absolutely essential quality if you are to survive or flourish. You must embrace forgiveness. However, the concept that forgiveness is one momentous event rather than a moment by moment choice places it out of the reach of most of us.

Learn to forgive what you are facing right now, without worrying about the future. For instance, if your spouse had an affair, sooner or later you will need to deal with the lies and deception, with the threats to your financial security, physical health and emotional stability. You'll need to face the risk posed to your children's stability, your social standing and on and on and on. Fortunately these don't all hit you at once or they would be overwhelming. Take them as they come, one at a time, hour by hour and you'll be surprised that God really does give grace for the moment. After all, that's all you have right now, just a moment, just one hour. So, choose to forgive for this hour, trusting that He'll help you with the next hour, when it gets here.

Stop The Clock

1. *Who came to your mind the moment you began reading this chapter?*

2. *What emotion was connected to their name?*

3. *What action does it require from you?*

4. *If you have a "tough forgiveness issue" in your life, ask God to help you forgive that person, for today. Deal with tomorrow when it comes. You might surprise yourself by entering a "path" of forgiveness.*

CHAPTER SIXTEEN

PEACE BY THE HOUR- Part 1
Analyzing The Anxiety Dragon

Worry occurs in every category of life: your job, your
health, your physical appearance, your family. You
probably even worry that you worry too much!

North Americans and Europeans are obsessed with worry. For decades we have carried on a love-hate relationship with folks from those parts of the world who practice siesta and regularly sip pina colada's while answering every request with, "Manana!" Perhaps the culminating commentary on the situation occurred in 1988 when Bobby McFerrin released his song, "Don't Worry, Be Happy!" Although it quickly rose to the top of the charts it never became clear whether its success was because it contained a much needed message or because we love to poke fun at people who live that way.

One would not be out of line to say that worry and anxiety is the number one problem in North America today. Do I overstate the case? Not likely. Fifty years ago Billy Graham wrote what is likely his most definitive book, <u>Peace With God</u>, in which he declared, "We are living in the age of anxiety. Historians tell us there have been few times in all history when man has been subject to so much fear and uncertainty." That was fifty years ago. Has it improved or deteriorated since then? I think we know the answer.

Occasionally when addressing audiences I ask them to turn to the person next to them and describe one thing they are worried about and why their worries are bigger than their neighbor's. It always results in nervous laughter but the bottom line is, no one is ever stumped for something to say. We are first rate worriers.

Dr. Dorothy McCoy says if you're a worrier, you should be worried. "Every system in your body is affected by worry. In addition to raising blood pressure and increasing blood clotting, worry can prompt your liver to produce more cholesterol, which in turn raises your risk of heart attack and stroke. It results in muscle tension which leads to headaches, back pain and other body aches. It triggers an increase in stomach acid and either slows or speeds up muscle contractions in your intestines which can lead to stomach aches, constipation, diarrhea, gas or heartburn." (McCoy, pioneerthinking.com). That's only the beginning, McCoy goes on to describe an even longer list of maladies related to worry. While McCoy deals with the physical issues, my favorite Bible teacher, John Ortberg, describes the internal results of worry. He says, "Anxiety cuts you off from the flow of the Spirit like almost nothing else. Worry robs me of joy, it makes me self-pre-occupied, less attentive or loving to others, makes temptations attractive because I want to escape inner pain, erodes my ability to feel grateful, increases my irritability …" (Ortberg, Willow Creek Messages CO314).

Anxiety is a dangerous dragon most of us spend huge portions of life wrestling with. *I don't know any part of life where the approach of Life By The Hour is more desperately needed than in the arena of anxiety.*

Because of the importance of this topic, I'm devoting two chapters to it. First we'll analyze the root causes of anxiety and then turn to some hour by hour anti-dotes.

Causes of Anxiety

Carrying the Weight of Past Defeats and Future Worries

You may want to go back and re-read the previous chapter. It is impossible to make it very far in life without accumulating baggage. That is just reality! However, we were never designed by the Creator to keep picking baggage up without ever setting it down. The result of not dealing with past sins, failures, defeats, hurts and pain is that they impact our ability to live positively in the present. Jesus says, "Each day has enough trouble of its own." If we insist on facing today with the weight of yesterday on our shoulders, today becomes undo-able.

The flip side of the coin is that many of us not only attempt to live today with yesterday's weight, but we add tomorrow's as well. We live in a constant state of, "What if?" What if I lose my job? What if my stocks go down? What if she has an affair? What if … what if … what if?

You were designed to be joyfully and fully alive today but if you insist on carrying the baggage of the past and the worry of tomorrow into today's agenda, the worry dragon will win.

Unrealistic Expectations

As ironic as it sounds, some people lose the battle because they worry about things that will never happen while others lose it because they are worrying about things that will happen anyway.

An amazing number of people stress out trying to avoid things that are inevitable. As a result, each little bump along the way destroys them. Each set back results in pity party complete with a band playing, "Why Is Everybody Always Picking On Me?"

The prophet Elijah had just won a huge victory for God. It was big. You can read about it in 1 Kings 18. But post-victory brought some problems. His life was threatened and in fear he ran, hid and got depressed. The Bible then records a debate with God in which Elijah says, "I'm the only one alive who still cares about God." Poor me. Do you re-call God's response? He said, "Yeah, right!" At least that's my paraphrase of it. Actually, He said, "Elijah, get real, there are at least 7000 others who have not bowed to Baal either."

Sometimes I feel like Elijah. I'm the only one, poor me. When I was 13-years-old I lost my job. I worked for the local hardware store. I'd go in every morning before school and sweep or shovel the sidewalk, then go back after school and sweep out the store. All for $6 a week. One day the boss came to me and said, "Tim, we're going to have to let you go." He said, "While you're shoveling or sweeping, the rest of the staff are just standing around. They could be doing it." I thought my world had come to an end.

Fired from my first job. Destined for a life of unemployment. I was only thirteen and didn't realize that guy was so cheap he just about cried every week he gave me the six bucks. And I didn't realize that layoffs are a fact of life.

Gather any group together and ask the following questions:

1. Have you ever either lost a job you wanted or had a job you didn't want?

2. Other than when you were born, have you ever been hospitalized?

3. Have you ever been in a car accident?

4. Have you ever had more bills than money?

5. Have you ever lost someone you loved, to death?

What you will discover in your survey is reality. Reality is that most of us will lose a job at some point; most of us will undergo a surgery or two; most of us will be in an accident; almost all of us will face financial challenges and, all of us will lose loved ones. These things are part of life. Yet we spend hours of energized time worrying that they might happen. Let me save you the worry time, *they will happen and they'll happen to you.*

A Need To Control

A third cause of anxiety is a need to control. The Gospel of Luke tells an interesting story of a visit by Jesus to the home of two sisters, Mary and Martha. Mary was spellbound by Jesus, sitting at his feet listening to him talk while Martha was consumed by hostess responsibilities. Finally, Martha couldn't take it anymore and gave Jesus a lecture for not making Mary help her.

Jesus' answer says it all. He said, "Martha, Martha ..."

Martha had a need for everything to be just perfect. She was filled with worry that there might be a fingerprint on a wine glass. Beyond that, she had a need for everyone to care about the same things she cared about.

It's hard to be joyful when you're wired that way. You worry not only about your life but about everyone else's too. Go very far down this path and you can be assured the dragon will win another round.

Overload

I'll state the obvious. You may be losing the battle with worry because you simply have too much on your plate. Every moment is filled with worry about what's coming next, because something always is.

From time to time in our home someone will have the popcorn maker going and someone else will be boiling the kettle to make tea and someone else will have the microwave on and I'll press the toaster down and guess what, the breaker goes. And my first tendency is to cuss the breaker, until I realize it is only doing its job.

It is possible that the breaker has flipped in your life so many times you've placed tape on the switch to make it easier to identify? Your doctor has warned you, your spouse has mentioned it, your kids have complained and your friends have expressed concern but you just keep going. Go too far and the dragon will win not only another round, he'll win the match.

If you are going to survive and flourish it's time to get ruthlessly honest about the role of anxiety in your life and deal with the root causes.

Stop the Clock

1. *This is not a chapter to rush. Re-read the 4 root causes of anxiety.*

2. *Which of the causes "rings true" with you?*

3. *How does it play out in your life?*

4. *Have those close to you provided feedback that indicates how it's impacting them too? What toll does it take on them?*

   Are you ready to slay the dragon? Read on ...

CHAPTER SEVENTEEN

PEACE BY THE HOUR – Part 2
Appropriating The Anti-Dote

I never cease to be amazed how many people pay the doctor
and then refuse to take the medicine!

> Warning: Mature Subject Matter!
> This chapter is for adults only.

Why the warning? Because if you think this chapter will provide some easy steps for victory over worry, you'll be deeply disappointed. This is the most rigorous, demanding chapter in the book.

I have a tough question for you. If you're still reading this far into the book I assume you are finding some benefit so give me the benefit of the doubt with this question. It's a serious question but one which, at first glance, you'll assume I'm asking tongue-in-cheek. Here goes:

"Do you really want to quit worrying?"

Think long and hard before you say, "Of course." Worry may be such a pattern in your life that getting rid of it will require major upheaval. Worry may be a means by which you gain a lot of attention and support. Do you still want to quit? Really?

If you do, you're going to have to really want it because it won't be an easy journey. In the previous chapter I referred to worry as a dragon. If anything I understated it. Worry is a dragon with the venom of a poisonous snake and the personality of a mamma grizzly bear separated from her cubs. It will destroy you if you don't destroy it. Do you still want to engage in the battle? It's an hour by hour fight. The dragon's primary weapon consists of two words, "What if?" Your anti-dote consists of five monster truths that you need to believe, rehearse and embrace on an hourly basis until they become as much a part of you as the color of your eyes. Without apology I am linking each of these monster truths to a scripture. I'm doing it on purpose. If you suffer from a serious battle with worry, I strongly encourage you to commit each of these Scriptures to memory. That won't be easy. They're not short or simple, but then again, what of value is?

Monster Truths That Will Slay The Dragon

I Am God's Prized Possession.

When our children were small we used to spend lots of evenings in park. One park has a large lagoon and owners of beautifully hand-crafted model boats would sail them via remote control radio. One night a storm came up and one of the models got swamped out in the middle of the lagoon. Within view of a large number of spectators, a grown man stripped down to his underwear and swam in after it. We were close enough to hear the conversation when he returned to shore. Someone asked him if he didn't find it embarrassing to strip to his underwear in front of dozens of strangers to retrieve a "toy" boat. His answer said it all. "That's my boat. I've invested hundreds of hours and hundreds of dollars in it, I'm not about to leave it out there."

With his words in mind, pay close attention to the following Scripture.

Isaiah 43:1-3 "But now, this is what the Lord says – he who created you, O Jacob, he who formed you, O Israel: "Do not fear, for I have redeemed you; I have summoned you by name, you are mine. When you pass through the waters, I will be with you; and when you pass through the rivers, they will not sweep over you. When you walk through the fire you will not be burned; the flames will not set you ablaze. For I am the Holy One of Israel, your Savior."

The order of these verses is critical. Many people tend to skip the first verse and delve right into the second. We do so to our own peril. "When we pass through the waters … when we pass through the rivers … when we walk through the fire." This is the list of the kinds of things most of us worry about! It's the stuff that overflows our soul. The Bible says, "Guess what? This is reality." The text is clear, it says, "when" not "if." You will face them. So, get real clear about it. The choice between peace and anxiety doesn't hinge on what might happen or what actually will happen. It isn't based on whether your circumstances are favorable or challenging. Sooner or later rough water and fiery blazes will be your reality. There is only one day you'll have no problems and that's the day they carry you out in a box. The key to peace is not freedom from negative circumstance it's embracing the ownership factor. Isaiah says you can face any circumstance because He created you; He formed you; He redeemed you; He called you by name. He says, *"You are Mine!"*

The first weapon in the arsenal is to refuse to deal with "what" you are worrying about until you have first dealt with "Whose" you are. The God of the universe says, "You're Mine!" Believe it, rehearse it and embrace it. God will not allow the waves to swamp you because He has a vested interest in you making it.

God Is Present

Several years ago when I was active in the police department my partner and I found ourselves in a back alley facing two very large, very ornery wanna-be prospects of an outlaw biker gang. They were not at all happy because of some action we had taken against them and they were about to act on their displeasure. It seemed probable to me that someone was going to get hurt and from all appearances it was going to be me and my rather small female partner. Fortunately I had two things on my side. First, I had already radioed for back-up; and second, I am a preacher who talks for a living (much better than I fight). So I said to our opponents, "Guys, here's the deal. You are going to jail for the night. That's non-negotiable. That will happen. Now, you look tough, most probably tougher than my partner and me, but, you can't beat everyone and 5 more cars will be here within 60 seconds." To my great joy and relief, they backed down and went to jail without incident.

It wasn't my bravery that won the day; it was my deep belief that help was on the way. If it wasn't, I probably would have put my marathon training into effect and run for my life. The bottom line is that issues are faced much differently when you are fully aware that sufficient help is on your side.

Hebrews 13:5-6: *God has said, "Never will I leave you; never will I forsake you." So we say with confidence, "the Lord is my helper; I will not be afraid. What can human beings do to me?"*

Take this truth to the extreme. Eliminate the word "I" from your vocabulary. Replace it with "WE." Get in the habit of saying as you head into that job interview, or doctor's office, or court room, or up to the teller's wicket, "God, if I had to go in there by myself, I'd go under, but if we go together, I'll be okay."

Practice living just one hour aware of God's presence. I'm confident the experience will lead to you looking forward to spending entire days, weeks and months that way.

I Am Under Construction

This morning was a tough start for me. I had a training run for an upcoming marathon and it was tougher than I either anticipated or wanted. To be honest I felt like staying in bed. Then, although I had the discipline to run, I felt like jogging instead of running hard. For the entire sixty minutes I kept repeating one phrase over and over in my mind. I said to myself, "This is preparing me for my goal."

How many times each day can you say that?

2 Cor. 4:16-17 *Therefore we do not lose heart. Though outwardly we are wasting away, yet inwardly we are being renewed day by day. For*

our light and momentary troubles are achieving for us an eternal glory that far outweighs them all."

There's enough truth here to chew on for months. Ask a friend who'll be honest with you to describe the best moment of their life. Chances are it will be a happy time. Then ask them to describe the time they grew the most. Inevitably they'll refer to a hard time. Ironically, we worry about and attempt to avoid the times that accomplish the most in us.

Each hour when the dragon knocks on your door, stare him down and tell him to bring it on because you would never want to miss out on something with the potential to accomplish so much good in you.

Peace Is A Mindset

The reason you won't like this dose of medicine is because none of us like being told we're responsible for our own problems. The reality is, until we accept responsibility for worrying, we'll never overcome it.

> *Ironically, we worry about and attempt to avoid the times that accomplish the most in us.*

The mind is a powerful thing. Proverbs says, "As a person thinks in their heart … so are they." The mind is like a river or stream out of which your life flows.

The human brain is constantly at work processing thousands of thoughts. This precise moment with this book in your hands you might simultaneously be thinking, "I don't like this chapter," only to notice your hands holding the book and the thought crosses your mind, "I'm still biting my nails, I wonder why," and then you tune in to a commercial on television and think, 'I've got to get that new detergent," and then you glance out the window and see a couple walk by holding hands and your marriage issues flutter to the surface.

Your mind is a stream. It's just like cable television with hundreds of channels all playing at once … *and you hold the remote. You get to choose which channel you're going to listen to.*

You are exposed to a constant barrage of thoughts. Some scholars have suggested that once a thought hits you, you have about one minute to root it out or it's got you.

Here's the Scripture for this Monster Truth: Romans 8:5 *"Those who live according to the sinful nature have their minds set on what that nature desires; but those who live in accordance with the Spirit have their minds set on what the Spirit desires."*

You can choose to fix your mind on things that are destructive and self-defeating or you can set your mind on things that lead to life and peace, under control of God's Spirit. You choose. The point is, you cannot "not" think about something. You can only choose your focus. It is futile to tell someone to stop worrying. No one has that power. What they can do is choose their focus, replacing destructive thought patterns with those that are productive and healthy.

Now, here's the clincher. You don't have to change your thinking forever more. Just for this moment. Just for these ten minutes. Then just for this hour. Yes you can! You can discipline your mind to stay focused on healthy thoughts for an hour … and if God helps you do it for this hour, you can trust Him for the next one. Hour by hour, you can slay the dragon. Believe it or not (and you might struggle with this), you can actually practice peace.

Peace Is A Gift

Finally, you catch a break. After being browbeaten with your role in the process I'm going to end by claiming that when everything is said and done, peace is a gift from God.

Philippians 4:6&7 *Do not be anxious about anything, but in every situation by prayer and petition, with thanksgiving, present your requests to God. And the peace of God, which transcends all understanding, will guard your hearts and your minds in Christ Jesus.*

It is critically important that you understand the nature of the gift. When you pray, when you trust God with your "stuff," it is vital that you grasp what He does and does not promise. This text provides absolute clarity that God does not promise a change of circumstances. If you pray about a financial worry St. Paul does not say you will suddenly get a check in the mail. When you pray about your marriage he doesn't suggest it immediately improves. So what is the gift? The peace of God ... will GUARD YOUR HEART AND YOUR MIND.

Worry attacks you at precisely those points. Worry attacks the part of you that processes life. St. Paul says when you choose to commit your anxieties to God in thankful prayer, He sends a guard, like the Roman garrisons Paul was so familiar with, to set up camp around your heart and mind. That's His gift.

Stop The Clock

The challenge of this chapter may very well occupy an entire month of your personal quiet time. IT WILL BE WORTH IT!

1. *Each day, read the verses listed in this chapter. If you don't get through them all don't worry. Stop whenever you find something meaningful.*

    ➢ *Isaiah 43:1-2*

    ➢ *Hebrews 13:5-6*

    ➢ *2 Corinthians 4:16-17*

    ➢ *Romans 5:8*

    ➢ *Philippians 4:6-7*

2. *Prayerfully ask God to teach you one truth each day.*

3. *Journal what you are learning.*

4. *Each week tell one person what you are discovering.*

CHAPTER EIGHTEEN
TEMPTATION BY THE HOUR
When You're Scared You Might...

Everyone faces demons — everyone!

I've had discussions with a murderer who killed a prostitute in a downtown hotel; a pastor who lost his career due to a dalliance with pornography; a father who molested his own daughter; a financial planner who embezzled hundreds of thousands of dollars; a wife who chose a fling over her family; and numbers of drunk drivers who killed or maimed innocent parties. Never once in all those discussions have I talked with someone who intended to wind up where they did. So, how does it happen?

I want to trace that process.

A year ago our daughter and her husband moved back to our city. Since she had a year of education to complete and since we have an in-law suite in our home, the decision of where they would live was simple until Lindsey reminded me they have a cat. I am not numbered among cat lovers. Everything with their move went better than I could have imagined with one exception. The cat has taken quite a shine to me. Why is it they always love the one person in the room who doesn't return the favor? She constantly begs to come upstairs to hang out, and will sit on my lap to watch an entire football game.

Recently our daughter announced that she has signed a one year contract to teach High School science … in China … and I inherit the cat! At that announcement I just sat in stunned silence wondering, "How did I wind up here?" How does someone like me become guardian of a cat?

I want to trace that process. How did Tiger Woods wind up a super star? How did Charles Manson wind up a mass murderer? How did you wind up where you are? How did Jesus Christ wind up on a cross?

Now, if you are able, just park that line of thinking for a minute, we're going to take a detour and then return to it.

Let me introduce a completely different topic. When is the last time you were lied to? Most of us can tolerate anything but lies, yet they happen all the time. "Nothing down, no interest, just 60 EASY payments." "No dieting, no exercise, for only minutes a day you can lose 5lbs a week." "Rub this stuff on your head and you too can re-grow a full head of hair." We're exposed to a constant barrage of claims of questionable truth.

One came my way recently. We returned home from vacation to discover our yard was infested with voles. Not moles, voles, those ugly, large field mice that tunnel in the grass. So I researched the problem, placed traps all over the yard, but then in a panic also went to the store and purchased a new, hi-tech, solar powered, pest-repeller. It claims to chase moles, gophers, voles and squirrels from your lawn and garden by emitting hi-pitched sounds. I assume, if it works, they'll move to our neighbor's yard, so success is a mixed blessing. It cost $29.95 However, I have my doubts about its effectiveness. I recently took a poll in a large audience and all but three people thought I'd just wasted $29. While commiserating over being lied to by the advertisers it suddenly hit me, it's okay because I now own a cat!

Okay, let's return to the parking lot where we were thinking about process, taking with us our new thoughts about lies. Here's the bottom line: At the heart of every temptation is a lie! And, if we buy the lie, it starts us down a path that will ultimately take us to a place we don't want to be.

An understanding of that process may very well be one of the most significant weapons in the arsenal to combat temptation.

First let's consider the most dangerous lies that lead us into temptation and covenant to censor them from our lives; and second, let's identify the kinds of truths we need to embrace hour by hour that will equip us to fight temptation when it comes.

At the heart of every temptation is a lie!

Lies That Need To Be Censored

In most first world countries censorship is a four letter word. It's too bad, because there are some lies that aren't appropriate for any audience. Here are four of the most dangerous:

It's Okay To Leave Some Wiggle-Room In My Commitments.

One of the saddest stories in the Older Testament of the Bible is the story of Solomon. At one point in his life he was arguably the wisest, richest, most "together" man ever to live. Yet, if you follow the story of his life you discover that he completely self-destructed. The seeds of his demise were sown years earlier. 1Kings 3 verse 3 includes a revealing comment about Solomon. *"Solomon showed his love for the Lord by walking according to the instructions given him by his father David, **except** that he offered sacrifices and burned incense in the high places."* Pay very close attention to the key word. You don't need to read any further and you don't need to know what comes next, that one word tells you trouble is knocking on the door. If you think I exaggerate, try this one at home tonight. Look at your spouse and say, "Honey, I love you and am faithful to you in every area except ..." It doesn't matter what fills in the blank, the blank itself predicts trouble. Commitment, by definition, is 100%. There is no such thing as partial commitment. Wiggle-room leaves the door open to disaster.

I mentioned earlier that my wife Arlene is a gastro-intestinal nurse. Every once in a while at the end of a busy day, if we have a dinner date or other commitment, she'll call me and say, "Tim, I'm sorry but I'm going to be late. We had a couple emergency add-ons and I still have to sterilize the scopes." And in full sensitivity I reply, "Can't you just do a quick job?" You know the answer. She says, patiently, as if explaining it to a backward child, "Tim, there's no such thing as a partially sterile scope. It's either sterile or it's not. If there's one germ alive, it's contaminated."

Most of us need to censor the lie that it's okay to leave the door to disaster open, as long as it's just a small crack. We allow ourselves to engage in "harmless" flirtations, little white lies, small indiscretions or soft porn, believing that as long as it's small it's okay. Where we deceive ourselves is in forgetting that it begins a process, it establishes a direction which, if left uncorrected, has a destination in mind.

I Am An Exception To The Rule.

What a lie! This pending disaster occurs when we agree with rules or principles for living but assume they are for others. Convincing ourselves that we're a bit smarter, a bit more sophisticated, that we can handle things most others can't, is as sure a formula for disaster as one can concoct.

We see this lie embraced every day. Smokers who know the facts but assume it'll never happen to them; over-eaters who have the truth readily available but continue to tip-toe through the trans-fat mine-field. The sad reality is, I do it too! We all do. One of the advantages of grey hair is that I've experienced just enough sin and failure in my life to know what dreadful things I'm capable of if I'm not careful. I've learned that I'm not immune, that I'm not an exception to the rules. So, in order to stay on track I need to fully engage in all the principles and safeguards possible or I'll lose the temptation war.

One day this was made clear to me was the day of my second marathon. Having run one marathon faster than my goal time, I was a little cocky as I prepared for my second. Sure I trained, but not with the intensity of the first one. After all, I was a veteran; I knew what it would take. Marathon day came and while I completed it, it was my worst marathon time ever. I remember talking to a 65+ year old lady in the recovery area, assuming she'd done the half marathon only to discover she had not only done the full marathon but she had kicked my butt by a significant margin. It was a valuable lesson for running, and even more valuable for living. Every time I've assumed that I'm above the rules, I've paid.

I Can Ignore What Doesn't Show.

Most of us remain quite ignorant in our understanding of temptation. Over and over I hear people bemoan, "If it had been any other temptation I could have withstood it." They fail to see that they have just defined "temptation." Temptations are personal and they are personally tailored. One of the root definitions of the word has its origin in the fishing industry. It means to design a lure. One doesn't go fishing and hang a million dollars or a naked girl or a chocolate chip cookie or a can of beer in the water. Lures are designed with each particular fish in mind. So are temptations, which is why knowing your predisposed weakness is of vital importance.

The real challenge of this arena is that most of our predisposed weaknesses are relatively private. Only we, or those very close to us know about them. It is their hidden nature that gives them such power. If you attend parties, I'm sure you've noticed that even heavy drinkers will usually be protective of a recovering alcoholic. Once a weakness is declared it loses the power of secrecy and isolation.

Censoring this lie involves two very courageous steps. First, it requires ruthless honesty with yourself; and, second, it involves confiding in a small group of people you trust. I'm not talking about hanging out your dirty laundry but I am recommending that you draw a few trusted friends into the struggle with you. Addressing your struggle with them has a double benefit. It dramatically lessens the hold temptation has over you and it enlists their support in holding you accountable.

You Have No Right To Tell Me What To Do.

This lie is so deeply ingrained in our culture I'm concerned even you might miss its importance. We have produced at least two generations on a steady diet of rights, privileges and freedoms. And we have created a monster! It is difficult to imagine any behavior which some group has not lobbied that it is their right to practice. Consequently, there is a strong tendency in all of us, when confronted with temptations, to convince ourselves that there is nothing wrong with giving in. It's my right. No one can tell me it's wrong. The capacity of the human mind to rationalize is incomparable!

In his letter to the Galatians, St. Paul suggests that one of the most mature practices anyone can engage in is that of correcting a fellow traveler when they get off course. The flip side is that one of the most mature attitudes anyone can have is a willingness to be corrected. Censor the lie that no one has the right to speak into your life. What they say may enable you to survive or to flourish.

Truths That Need To Be Embraced

Nothing exists in a vacuum! Refusing to believe lies is only half the equation. The second half involves focusing on what you deeply believe? These truths merit consideration.

You Are Not As Unique As You've Been Told

Forgive me for stating a positive truth in a negative way. There are times in life to emphasize your individuality and uniqueness but the midst of temptation is not one of them. The definitive Bible verse on temptation is 1 Corinthians 10:13. Three of these five truths emerge directly from it. St. Paul says, *"No temptation has overtaken you except what is common to us all..."* The tendency in temptation is to convince yourself that you are the only one who has ever struggled with it. That gives the temptation inordinate power over you. If you truly believe that no other married human being has ever been attracted to someone other than their spouse you'll be convinced that your attraction is something special. If you believe that the thoughts you struggle with are unique to you, you'll be convinced that something is radically wrong with you for thinking them. The result in either case is that you empower the temptation and position yourself to cave in. The truth is that these are just run of the mill temptations that are common to thousands of people all the time. If they can overcome them, so can you.

There Is A Way Out.

The same Bible verse ends this way. *"But when you are tempted, he will also provide a way out so that you can endure it."* Greg Hochhalter is a friend and colleague who I once asked to teach an entire session on temptation. He did a masterful job of capturing this truth through one picture. If you live on the prairies it may be foreign to you, but those of us in mountain regions get it immediately. On mountain highways, prolonged downhill slopes always include what is known as a "Run Away Lane." If the driver of an eighteen wheeler has blown his or her air brakes and missed a downshift or two, a downhill, curvy highway means certain disaster. So, highway engineers include strategically placed exits which lead to an uphill slope so drivers can get their rig stopped. Greg read this truth, and then did a power point presentation of various run away lanes. What a powerful truth. With every temptation, God provides an escape route. If you embrace this truth, when you are tempted, instead of focusing on the power of the temptation you can focus on finding the escape route you know is there.

You Can Win This One!

Yes you can! Back to the verse. *"God is faithful; he will not let you be tempted beyond what you can bear..."* The most common lie in the middle of a temptation is, "I can't." Yes you can! God says so. And remember, you don't have to win every temptation today, just the one you're facing. You only need to win this hour.

Sports clichés get tiresome after a while, but the reason they become clichés is because they communicate something important. Coach after coach when interviewed will say, "We don't have to worry about all the remaining games, just tonight's game. In fact, we don't need to worry about the whole game, just one shift, or one at bat or one play at a time." Exactly! If you've got an eating disorder, you don't have to keep every meal down, just this one. Or, you don't have to lose 100 lbs, just one more. It's amazing how temptations lose their hold on you when you break them down and believe God has promised that "THIS ONE" you can win.

You Are Loved

If you are knowledgeable about the Bible, you'll probably know that the temptations of Christ occurred immediately after his baptism. That is very significant. Two of the three temptations use the phrase, "if you are the Son of God," and are intended to raise doubt. The importance of understanding the sequence is that at the time of His baptism, a voice from heaven declared, "You are My beloved Son, in whom I am well pleased." Setting out on his divine mission, fully aware of who he was, made Jesus dangerous, so the adversary attacked his identity.

The same approach is included in almost every temptation. Temptations are designed to communicate the lie that you are not close to the Father. You are evil, you are distant, you are alone. I believe the greatest power there is to win the temptation battle is the power of knowing that God is close and in love with you. Your identity as His beloved child will keep you from more wrong decisions than you can count.

Censor the lies and embrace the truths. Remember, everyone faces demons but by God's grace they can be defeated.

Stop The Clock

1. So, what is your "lie of choice?"

    a. Wiggle room is ok

    b. I'm the exception

    c. It doesn't show

    d. I have my rights

2. What truth do you need to allow to seep into your innermost being?

    a. you're not that unique

    b. there is a way out

    c. you can win

    d. you are deeply loved

3. To whom have you given permission to ask you the tough questions and to speak truth into your life?

4. If no one comes to mind, consider inviting 2 trusted friends to join you in an accountability group.

CHAPTER NINETEEN

GRIEF BY THE HOUR: WHEN LIFE IRREVOCABLY CHANGES

Part of learning how to live is knowing you're going to die.

There are only two kinds of people in the world: Those who are facing the reality discussed in this chapter today and those who will face it tomorrow. But face it we will. Coming to terms with the death of people we love and coming to terms with our own mortality is a journey we all take.

I'm not sure whether it's truth or urban legend but for years I've heard the story of a pastor (I've heard different pastors described), who was on a flight where a little girl suddenly became very ill and died. It was a tragic and traumatic experience for everyone involved. The airplane made an immediate, emergency stop where she was removed from the plane at which time the flight continued. Once back in the air the pastor summoned one of the flight attendants and said to her, "I just want you to know that I'm a minister and if anyone in the immediate area is having difficulty coping with this I'd be happy to talk with them and offer whatever help I can."

"Oh," she said, "I think they'll be alright. We've given them free drinks."

We don't live in an era where, generally speaking, people face the ultimate issue of life and death very well. Even the concept of heaven is shrouded in confusion and myth. We use the term "heaven" or "heavenly" to describe almost anything that is – nice. I recently saw an advertisement for the "Nearly Heaven Spa and Hot Tub Company." It's the theme for countless numbers of songs, Christian and otherwise: "Knock, Knock, Knockin On Heaven's Door," or Eric Clapton's, "Tears In Heaven."

Perhaps worst of all, heaven is the brunt of an endless stream of jokes. Out of any ten jokes, at least one or two will be about someone dying and winding up at the pearly gates giving rise to all sorts of silliness.

The tragedy of the issue, however, is that for all the attention it receives, the concept of dying and going to heaven remains one of life's most badly misunderstood issues. I recently came across a survey reported in USA Today that showed the level of ignorance on this topic. 88% of American adults said they were certain they were going to heaven. However, in a different question, only 67% declared they were certain there is a heaven. It sort of makes you wonder where the other 21% believe they're going.

Where do you rate yourself on the coping scale for this, the ultimate challenge? Jokes and meaningless banter are okay until the reality of death makes its way into your home. Then you need more.

Let me offer four provisions for the ultimate reality. As you've come to expect by this point in the book, none of them is a provision you accept "once and for all." They are daily, hourly, moment by moment provisions to help you both survive and flourish in the face of the final challenge. If you are facing grief today, my prayer is that these provisions will give you a glimpse of life beyond your pain.

Provision 1: Confident Hope

I have chosen these words carefully because I want to make a sharp distinction between what I'm saying and "wishful thinking." Ask some people if they're going to heaven when they die and the answer you will receive is, "I sure hope so." But it's said without conviction. Provision #1 is a Confident Hope.

1 Peter 1:3-4 puts it this way: *"Praise be to the God and Father of our Lord Jesus Christ! In his great mercy he has given us new birth into a living hope through the resurrection of Jesus Christ from the dead, and into an inheritance that can never perish, spoil or fade, kept in heaven for you..."*

I'm not a great historian and I don't want to bore you with ancient detail, but the context in which these verses were written is essential. It is most likely that this text was written around 67AD which puts it just after the first major round of persecution by Nero. These words were written from a heart of encouragement to people who'd gone through the fire and for who even worse things were poised on the horizon. These are ultimate words.

In that context Peter says to those he loved, when the fire gets the hottest, remember this: First, God is not distant or unknowable. He's the Father of our Lord Jesus. Second, His primary characteristic is mercy. Not judgment, not wrath, but mercy, great mercy. These hard times of suffering are not because God is mad or judging as we so often believe but rather, hard times call out God's mercy. Third, remember He has given us a new birth. It's a birth that is closely connected to the resurrection. This is an Easter faith. Fourth, this promise is our inheritance. Today we speak of an inheritance as a future possession. In Bible times the word meant a secure possession that could not be taken away by Nero or by death, because, it was kept in heaven.

The confident hope is that God has an inheritance for you in a place where only you can get it. Nero can't touch it.

So, if you're facing the giant of death today, either your own or that of someone you deeply love, the first provision God offers is a hope which nothing can touch.

Provision 2 – Realistic Expectations

I've quoted the Bible liberally throughout this book. One reason I'm so high on it is because it's so real. The scriptures don't sugar coat life. They record real life and real death.

Personally, I have little use for people who offer platitudes and clichés in moments when my heart is crushed. I know they mean well, but assuring someone who is facing ultimate reality that everything will be just fine, somehow rings hollow.

St. Paul doesn't do that. Consider this common text on dying. It's from 2 Timothy 4. *"For I am already being poured out like a drink offering, and the time for my departure is near. I have fought the good fight, I have finished the race, I have kept the faith. Now there is in store for me the crown of righteousness, which the Lord, the righteous Judge will award to me on that day – and not only to me, but also to all who have longed for his appearing."*

If you have attended a Christian funeral, you've heard these verses. Many focus only on Paul's positive attitude. They fail to notice that he refers to it as "being poured out like a drink offering." Many focus on the positive terms of being set free to win the prize. What they miss is that you only win the prize after fighting the fight, finishing the race and keeping the faith. Most seem to think these are terms from the arena of Olympic sports. You don't get the crown without first enduring the contest. I love the realism. Paul is positive in his view of what will happen but he never denies the toughness of the course to get there.

I am of no help to you if I attempt to pretty up death. We do have a confident hope but the leaving portion is just hard for everyone.

You may feel that no one understands your pain if this is your reality today. The Bible does. It refuses to gloss over the depth of the journey.

Provision 3 – A Motivating Promise

Which has a bigger attraction to you, if I tell you I have an incredible surprise for you or if I tell you I'll give you a hundred dollars. Most of us are far more compelled by the surprise.

1 Corinthians 2:9 *"However, as it is written: What no eye has seen, what no ear has heard, and what no mind has conceived – these things God has in prepared for those who love Him."*

The reason there is so much speculation about heaven is because no one knows exactly what to expect. With all due respect to those who claim to have been there and back, we're given just enough hints in the Bible to know that it is going to be greater and grander and more unbelievable than anything we could imagine. The descriptions, I believe, are to whet our appetites. God says I have a really great surprise for you, just wait.

Provision 4 – A Compelling Vision

At the heart of most of the descriptions of heaven in the Bible are these core concepts. God will be given His rightful due; wrongs and injustices will be righted; sorrow and suffering will disappear.

Just imagine!

So, the final question is, "Is this stuff real?" "Does it make an actual difference when facing the ultimate reality?" This exact moment while I sit at my keyboard writing these words, one of my colleagues returned from a funeral. An administrative assistant asked him, "How was the funeral?" His reply was, "I've never seen a more meaningful celebration, with tears."

I hope that will describe all my encounters with grief. Reality faced, hope claimed. Yes, it's real!

Stop The Clock

1. *Think about conversations you've been involved in that have focused on the topic of death. What words would you use to describe them? (morbid, fearful, hopeful, philosophical)*

2. *How did the concept of heaven play into those conversations – if at all?*

3. *If you, or someone you loved were diagnosed with a terminal illness, where would you turn for comfort?*

Important Note: Chapter 24 is a must read chapter for anyone wrestling with life's ultimate question.

PART FIVE

DON'T JUST SURVIVE – FLOURISH!

CHAPTER TWENTY
Living The Formula

Whatever you do, work at it with all your heart as working
for the Lord, not for human masters. (Col. 3:23)

Another way of stating that verse is this:

$$nc + din + pfk + kw = yb$$

Have you ever sat on the sofa watching a group of extreme athletes perform a death defying feat and wondered out loud, "Are they nuts?" I have. But I've also watched those scenes and wondered, "Why not?" And speaking of being "nuts," what honestly makes more sense, living on the edge or sitting on the sofa watching others live it on television?

Let me pose a rather predictable question but think carefully before you answer because while the question may be predictable the answer you give is far from run-of-the-mill. It's unbelievably hi-stakes! Here's the question: (and this is not an age-graded question, it applies equally to 8-year-olds as it does to 34-year-olds or 81-year-olds) Is it possible that just in front of you may lay the most exciting or extreme adventure you've ever been part of? As you look at the blank squares on the calendar, whether it's next week, next month or next year, do you view those squares with eager anticipation of what God may invite you to participate in or do you have a sense of resignation that your best accomplishments are either already behind you or are so far in front of you there's no use getting your hopes up? Do you live with a sense of dread, accepting that everything of real significance has already taken place so you're just going to mark in the squares with less and less meaningful activities until the day you die? Or do you assume that your life-stage is such that your very best years are significantly out of reach, 3-6-7-15 years away and you're going to have to fill time until you get to the stage where you can engage in something of real value? Or, do you look at the open space in front of you and wonder what incredible thing God might have in mind for you this year?

I'm going to stir the controversy pot, not for controversy sake but for your sake. I believe the attitude you hold and the answers you give to those questions are THE most important decisions you'll make today. You get to chose how you view your life and your future. And it starts this hour and proceeds every hour hereafter.

The trap many of us fall into is to view life *"in comparison."* Instead of standing before God with our hands and hearts and wills and minds open, saying, "Father, what call do You have for me this hour that I can follow with a sense of eager expectation," we compare our lives with others or with other life stages, past or future. We then conclude that we can't really do much that compares anyway, so back to the sofa, and please pass the afghan.

Whenever I talk in these terms I think of Errol. Errol is my friend. He's a middle-aged man who found a relationship with God just a few years ago and experienced a radical life-change, but then ran into serious health issues which included losing his leg. For a period of time he struggled. Was there anything of worth in the empty spaces of his life? Then he started asking the right questions, the questions I've posed to you, such as, "What do You have for me now Lord?" and although the next chapters of his life remain to be written, he got back on the horse and recently placed 10th overall in the Canadian Body For Life Challenge. Not in a contest for amputees but competing against everyone else with two legs. He could have stayed on the sofa and no one would have blamed him. Now, using the platform of his accomplishment, Errol and his wife have launched a group called Faith and Fitness in which he builds into the lives of others who aren't sure they can make it.

When I wonder out loud whether God might have an incredible chapter $$nc + din + pfk + kw = yb$$ just ahead in the spaces of my calendar, I'm not suggesting I either have to discover the cure for cancer or it doesn't count. Rather, I'm posing the question of whether this hour, this week, or this year I'm open to whatever call God has for me that might take me into waters I've never explored before. The reason I said this is your decision is because I believe to my core that God has already planned for it to happen if you'll just agree with Him!

Now for the formula that will help you make it happen:

$$nc + din + pfk + kw = yb$$

The formula is an analysis of the verse I've chosen as my life verse. I'll repeat the verse and then break down the formula for you. In fact I encourage you to memorize it; it's so powerful you'll want it on the tip of your tongue. *Whatever you do, work at it with all your heart, as working for the Lord, not for human masters. (Colossians 3:23)*

Here's the analysis.

nc = no compartments

What part of life are you to approach "with all your heart?" My life verse says, "Whatever you do." There are no exceptions, no compartments. If you are accustomed to studying the Bible you know the value of understanding the context. The context of this verse is crucial. Paul has just discussed relationships in the church. He gets so specific he says that even how enthusiastically you sing, matters. Then he addresses wives, then husbands, then children, then fathers, then slaves (today we would say employees), then masters or employers. Think about it, in church, in your marriage, in your family, at work, in WHATEVER YOU DO!!

The problem is that very few people actually believe this. A heresy has plagued Christianity from its earliest days. It's a heresy that suggests life can be divided into neat compartments. Most often they are labeled, "Sacred" and "Secular," and behind those labels many put the descriptors "*Good*" and "*Bad*." Instead of learning to live well and to honor God with ALL life, with our WHOLE being, instead of serving Him in "whatever we do," we've convinced ourselves that God really only cares about one compartment, so we can slack off in the others. BIG problem!

There's a reason I've selected this verse as my life verse. My uncle, Gary Schroeder was killed in an accident in Cameroon, Africa while working as a missionary. The agency he worked for presented the family with a citation, written in his honor. Today it hangs in a place of prominence in my den. It bears these words:

With deepest sense of gratitude we present this citation in loving memory of the Reverend Gary Schroeder who gave himself WHOLLY to the task God had set before him. His desire to present the Cameroonians the whole gospel was always evident. Though he was removed from the scene by death his ministry continues as many remember his ENTHUSIASM for the Lord's work and are motivated to increase their own devotion. Our deepest tribute to him is that his life reflects God's words; whatever you do, work at it with all your heart as working for the Lord and not for men.

After Gary was killed, a fellow missionary told us that he had the honor, along with several Cameroonians to build the casket Gary was buried in. In that culture you don't go to the funeral home, you make things yourself. The missionary said, "I was nailing the casket together and bent a nail. I drove it in and went on. One of the Cameroonians came behind me, pulled out the crooked nail and drove one in straight. All he said was, 'Gary would never approve of a crooked nail.'"

Whatever you do; whether it's pounding nails or making lunch; whether the boss is watching or away on vacation; when you pay your employees or play with your kids; whatever you do, do it with your whole heart. No compartments!

din = do it now

The verse says, "Whatever you DO." This is not for couch potatoes, arm chair quarterbacks or critics. This is for doers.

When this verse first became meaningful to me I decided to take it apart and put it under the microscope. I started by trying to study the word – DO. I assumed it would be a simple task. What I found is that the Greek word we translate "do" had more than thirty pages of definition beginning with God creating the world. "Doing" is apparently a very important biblical word.

There's been a lot of talk in the last few years about "being" instead of "doing." It's a meaningful concept except for one problem: you can't separate the two. Sooner or later who you are finds expression in what you do. So, what does it say if you do nothing or do nothing with passion? It says that instead of a calling that possesses you, instead of passion that overflows your soul, you have a hollowness or emptiness inside.

If God provides an opportunity and a nudging to seize it, for God's sake and yours, DO something.

pfk = play for keeps

"Whatever you do, work at it with ALL your heart."

This is diametrically opposed to what you've been taught most of your life. You've been taught, "Don't put all your eggs in one basket." You've been taught, "Have a diversified portfolio." That's probably good investment advice, but it is lousy living advice. The question is, and it's really the question of life, "Do you have anything worth giving your whole life to?" Do you have a calling that deserves your passion? Do you have such an understanding of Who God is and Who He's made you to be and are living in such confidence that what you're involved in is what He wants you involved in that you can dare to do it with ALL your heart?

Making that discovery isn't something anyone else can do for you, that's your job!

Have you cultivated the habit of giving your whole heart? When you're with your spouse do they get all of you or just the leftovers? When you're at work or school does it gets your best energy? When you're at play, are you fully engaged? When you're parenting are you fully present? When you worship, do you worship full out? When you pray do you get gut-wrenchingly honest and pour out your whole heart to God? Most of us need to learn to play for keeps far more often than we do.

kw = know why

Know why. Don't you dare give your whole heart, unless you know why. "Whatever you do, work at it with all your heart as working for the Lord and not for man."

As a pastor I regularly ask people to make huge sacrifices. I ask them for their time, their talents and their money. Over the years I've learned that if I'm going to ask someone to sacrifice I have to know why. Often, after concluding Christmas Eve services (it has not been uncommon for us to hold 4, 5 or 6 services) I marvel at the number of people who volunteer to make it happen. From those who passionately use their musical or dramatic talents to those who freeze their butts off directing traffic, hosting Christmas services at a large church requires hundreds of volunteers. And I watch hundreds of people every year give their Christmas to make it happen. Why? Why would anyone do that? As I've wrestled with that question I've concluded that I don't know even one of them who would do it if it was only to make Christmas Eve nice. Rather, it's because somewhere deep down inside we've come to believe that God uses special moments to open doors to people's hearts and that somewhere down the road we'll hear stories from people whose lives were dramatically changed and they'll say, "I first got interested in God at a Christmas Eve program. I started on a journey that night and my life has been forever changed." For that, people will sacrifice.

Whatever you do, work at it with all your heart as working for the Lord, not for human masters. If you do, it's possible that this next hour may just happen to be *yb*, which by the way = your best.

Stop The Clock

1. *Is there any evidence in your life that you have a tendency to divide life into compartments? If so, what contributes to it and how can you eliminate it?*

2. *Which part of the formula do you resonate best with?*

(nc – din – pfk – kw)

3. *Which do you struggle with most? Can you think of any reasons this part is so difficult for you?*

CHAPTER TWENTY ONE

Praying By The Hour:
Never Face Life Alone

Adventurous prayer remains life's greatest mystery.

There are two words I want to explore with you. The first is "token." You know what it means. If you're a journeyman plumber or seamstress and you do $500 worth of work for a friend and they hand you a card and say, "This is a token of our appreciation," what it means is that instead of the $500 you could have earned doing the same work for anyone else, you'll probably find a $10 Starbucks card inside. That's a token. Or, if there's a committee established with a mandate to have seven members and the first six selected are all women and you're a man and they ask you to be the final member, no matter what else they may tell you, you are a token. You're a lucky token, but a token nevertheless.

The second word I want to explore is, "Adventure." When you fully throw yourself into something with no reservation, even if it involves risk or danger, it's an adventure.

Quick test: Is sky diving a token sport or an adventure? How about Tidily-Winks?

With these two words on the front burner of your mind, let's get serious. Does prayer occupy a token place in your life or is it an adventure? The reason this question is of such significance is because if prayer occupies only a token place in your life, you may not only be settling for less than God intended for you, but you may get accustomed to life on that level. It is possible to actually live one's entire life as a token and never fully experience a flourishing adventure. But that's not God's intent. God invites us to a state of constant communication with Him resulting in life on a different plane.

One of my favorite Bible accounts is found in the Book of Acts chapter 12. It describes the mysterious relationship between praying and the action of God. And, it raises the question, "How can I make sure I move beyond token prayers and get on the adventure side?" If I want my life to flourish, how do I pray accordingly?

To be blunt, I believe most of us have had it with token praying: token praying in public, token praying in church, and especially token praying in our own lives. And we are starved for the adventure. So, if you resonate at all with that let's consider how we can inject some adventure into our prayers.

Acts 12 describes several dimensions to adventurous praying.

Prayer Defines Your Reality.

Is what you see all there is to life? Do your problems define what's real, or is there more? Prayer defines your reality.

Acts 12: 1-6 *It was about this time that King Herod arrested some who belonged to the church, intending to persecute them. He had James, the brother of John, put to death with the sword. When he saw that this met with approval among the Jews, he proceeded to seize Peter also. This happened during the Festival of Unleavened Bread. After arresting him, he put him in prison, handing him over to be guarded by four squads of four soldiers each. Herod intended to bring him out for public trial after the Passover. So Peter was kept in prison, but the church was earnestly praying to God for him. The night before Herod was to bring him to trial, Peter was sleeping between two soldiers, bound with two chains, and sentries stood guard at the entrance.*

Let me underscore the core facts of this story.

First, this King was Herod Agrippa I, the grandson of Herod the Great. You might remember from the Christmas story that this is the family who slaughtered all the baby boys born around the time of Jesus' birth? This is the family who had people killed when one of their family members died because they wanted to be sure there would be crying. This was an absolutely ruthless regime. The Herods would stop at nothing. So, to win favor with the Jews and keep peace in the land, Herod started killing Christians. James, the one we always see listed with Peter and John had already been killed, probably beheaded, and when the public opinion polls soared because of that, Herod grabbed Peter as well and threw him in jail. The text then goes into considerable detail about how Peter was guarded. Why, because earlier in the story (Acts 5) Peter and John had already pulled one prison break. So this time there was nothing left to chance. Herod would not be embarrassed. Peter was in jail with 16 soldiers guarding him, 4 at a time in shifts. He was doubly chained. Most prisoners were chained only to one guard, he was chained on both sides and sentries were posted at the door.

The text goes on to say that Herod intended, as soon as the feast was over the next morning, to bring Peter out. The word literally means, for a "SHOW TRIAL." He was going to bring him out for public display, to make an example of him.

Those are the cold, hard facts. On one side you have all the authority of Herod, the power of the sword, and the very best security money could buy. On the other side you have what? What was the other reality? What did the early church have to put up against all that? Only one thing: prayer.

What difference does prayer make? Part of the answer is found in verse six. I absolutely love this verse, "*The night before Herod was to bring him to trial, Peter was sleeping between two soldiers...*"

I think the biggest transformation in Peter's life as he grew with God was not that he could preach or lead, it was that he could sleep. He'd become aware of another reality.

Have you? Is the reality of your life just what you can see and touch and prove in a laboratory ... or is there *another* reality, rooted in intimate conversation with your Heavenly Father?

Quite a few years ago I was speaking in Sioux Falls, SD and I went to visit my aunt who was dying of cancer. I won't bore you with the details of my extended family relationships other than to say she occupied a very special place in our family and there she was in the final stages of her battle. She couldn't talk very well anymore but we visited and prayed together and then, as I had my hand on the door to leave, knowing I'd likely never see her again, she said, "Tim," and I turned back, and she said, "See you in heaven."

She was living in another reality. There was the oxygen mask and the pain and the medicine, that was one reality, but she chose another one.

When you pray, when you really pray, you're not visiting fantasy land, you're engaging another reality. You're not denying this life with all its challenges and hurts and pains but you are declaring that your hope and trust is in the reality of your Father God, Whom you trust with your whole life.

That kind of insight isn't something that occurs once in your life; it's an hour by hour pursuit.

Prayer Reveals Your Devotion.

There's another significant word in this story, found in verse five. *"So Peter was kept in prison, but the church was earnestly praying to God for him."*

Earnestly! It means to stretch out like an athlete diving to make a catch, with intensity, and fervency. Some translate it un-remittingly. What grabs me about this word is that it's the same word used in Luke 22 to describe how Jesus prayed in the Garden of Gethsemane where it says his sweat became like drops of blood.

This was not "token" prayer.

I am going to admit something you might find strange. After all I am a pastor and you might expect that I should know all about this, but to be completely honest, I haven't got a clue how prayer works. I know some people write books and claim to understand it, but prayer remains one of the great mysteries to me.

How it is that Almighty God is moved by the prayers of people like me? There's only one explanation I can think of and that's that He loves me so deeply that when I am fervent and earnest in calling to Him, His heart is touched. It's for sure not a magic formula, that if I pray for something three times I'm more likely to get it than if I only pray once, or if I pray really loudly God will answer more than if I whisper. It's nothing like that, yet somehow, in God's economy, earnest prayers make a difference.

Prayer Challenges Your Expectations.

I don't know how else to describe this part of the story other than to say it's just flat out hilarious. This is some of the best humor in the Bible.

The miracle happened. An angel came, poked Peter in the ribs and told him to get up and get dressed. Pete thought he was dreaming but nevertheless obeyed. He got out onto the street, realized it wasn't a dream and headed off to Mary's house where the church prayer meeting was being held. Verse 13 says all that needs to be said on this topic. "*Peter knocked at the outer entrance, and a servant named Rhoda came to answer the door. When she recognized Peter's voice, she was so overjoyed she ran back without opening it and exclaimed 'Peter's at the door!'*"

And the whole time Peter, a fugitive from prison, was left standing at the door. You've got to visualize it: Peter, looking over his shoulder for soldiers in pursuit, whispering hoarsely, "Rhoda, Rhoda you nimwit, let me in." I suspect a few terms from when he was a fisherman might have come to mind. Speaker John Ortberg, tongue in cheek says, "I've done extensive study on the root word for the name Rhoda, it means 'blond.'" He was just kidding, I think. But, the text says, because of her joy, because of her uncontrolled emotion; she left him on the step.

Then it gets worse. The group inside didn't believe her. Verse 15 "'You're out of your mind,' they told her. When she kept insisting that it was so, they said, 'It must be his angel.'"

Don't miss this; it could happen in any church today. There they were, earnestly praying, likely risking their lives to pray, but when God answered their prayer they didn't believe it.

Verse 16, "But Peter kept on knocking, and when they opened the door and saw him – they were astonished."

You know why we laugh when we read this text? It's called a defense mechanism. Prayer challenges expectations.

As I've grown older and hopefully more mature, I have done more praying and had more answers to prayer than at any time in my life. I've had specific moments when I've been stuck, really stuck in message preparation and have asked God very specifically for creative thoughts, and have been astonished when thoughts come. I've prayed for things for our family, very specifically and have seen God far exceed what I ever hoped for. I've prayed in a sustained manner for people God brings to my mind, and have watched Him do wonderful things for them. And yet, so often I continue to act like Rhoda. I've been so used to token praying that I only expect token responses and when God gives adventurous responses, I'm shocked. But I'm learning. Are you?

From the opening pages this book has been about two stories. It's been about the story of a young man who couldn't see his way clear to continue living and it's been about the story of

Oscar, who still needed to earnestly pray on the last day of his life. It's been about two words, Survival and Flourishing. I want to tell you with all the honesty I can summon, the key difference between the two stories and the two words is found in a relationship with God that leaves token living in the dust and counts on adventurous praying.

Stop The Clock

1. *This is an obvious question but it needs to be asked. Which of the two words best describes your prayer life, token or adventure?*

2. *Have there been moments in your life when you've been particularly conscious of another reality? Think about the circumstances that led you to be that aware.*

2. *When you pray, do you actually expect God to answer?*

   a. *Make a point when you pray to clarify that you aren't just talking, you are asking God to be involved in your life and you fully expect that He will.*

   b. *When He answers your prayers, keep track of the answers and be sure to say thanks.*

   c. *When you pray expectantly, keep track of answers and give thanks, watch how token praying faces and the adventure begins.*

CHAPTER TWENTY TWO
Navigating The $ Forest

Dollars may not burn a hole in your pocket but
chances are they'll burn a hole in your soul.

A recent phenomenon has taken North America by storm. It's nothing new, only old stuff in a new package.

The Secret, in the DVD version, rose quickly to #1 position on the Amazon chart and the book held either #1 or #2 spot at Amazon, Barnes & Noble, Borders and USA Today for most of early 2007.

The Secret is based on the law of attraction that says, "If you think positively you become a magnet that pulls everything you want toward you." You can have it all, if you only believe.

Is that true? Or is it part of a belief system that's taken us into the greedy mess we're in? Only one year ago, some would have taken me to task for describing our age as a greedy mess. Today, no one argues that description. If you think it's even a slight exaggeration, think about this: for a time last year, Apple had a download that you could install on your iPhone ... that glows. That's it. It costs $999 and it glows. Its purpose? To prove to your sports cronies, business rivals, or guys and gals you're trying to impress that you are rich and can afford a $1000 glowing icon on your phone. It's a thousand dollar, "I Am Rich" sticker. They actually sold a few before pulling it off the market.

I've described the extreme on purpose. It's so that for at least a couple minutes you could relax and feel superior and say to yourself, "I'd never do THAT!" Because I suspect for at least part of the rest of this chapter you might have to say, "Ouch." At least I did as I wrote it.

Let's shift from such unbelievable extravagance, to the extravagance we live with on a daily basis. Would it be a fair statement to say that the city you live in is "financially charged?" That money matters? It's true of my city.

I noticed a change a couple of years ago while on an airplane. I remember a time when I would read the airline magazines and they would show extravagant places around the world like Paris and the Caribbean. Well in the last couple years I've noticed that a lot of those ads now feature my city, Kelowna. And the prices are what used to be in Paris?

Drive into Kelowna today and you'll see a billboard advertising a development with homes starting at a mere three million dollars. There have always been extravagant homes in the valley; no one gives that a second thought. But think about a highway billboard advertising homes for the average person, at three million dollars. I remember buying our first house in Kelowna for less than a hundred thousand dollars and wondering, "Will we ever be free of this?"

And it's not just the housing market, every day conversations focus on season tickets for sporting events, ski passes, golf club memberships, boats, motorcycles, motor-homes, winter vacations and winter homes. I'm not saying it's all bad, and I have to admit I'm part of at least some of it, but it underscores the fact, we live in a very financially charged day. And, at the same time this is happening, on the other side of the equation there are hundreds who can't find a place to live they can afford. These are working people I'm talking about. And back when I started writing this book, who would have guessed what the stock market would do in 2008 and 2009, or gasoline prices which have some us of reverting to our teenage habit of planning strategically which day we might be able to afford a full tank of gas.

Now for the big question: What does any of this have to do with you? What does it have to do with Life By The Hour? What does it have to do with being a follower of Jesus Christ? The answer: everything. Few forces have greater power to mess up your life in every dimension than financial pressure.

As I wrote this chapter I struggled with my reason for doing so. I'm not a financial planner, strategist or wizard. Then part way through the writing, it hit me, and hit me hard. I don't need to be a financial strategist. That's not my role. I'm a pastor with a genuine concern for people. This is all about wanting to nudge you and help you navigate a course in this financially charged day that will keep you from self-destruction; a course that will position you to one day stand before God and not have to shrink in embarrassment because of the way you've handled your resources.

Special Note: Between the writing of the first draft of this chapter and today, financial disaster has struck not only most of North America but most of the world. If ever there is proof positive of the importance of this subject, we are now living in it. And yet, in the midst of lay-offs and re-possessions, many are proposing the solution is for us to spend even more. Hello!!!

Let me suggest four determinations you can make which will help you navigate your way through the $ forest regardless which part of the financial spectrum you find yourself in.

First, determine to address the power money has over you. The natural tendency of every one of us is to think this applies to someone else. The wealthy think it applies to the poor who are consumed with money because they don't have any and the poor think it applies to the wealthy because they've chased it so energetically. Then there are those in the middle who think it applies to both the rich and the poor but not to the middle class — we're the normal ones. We are all wrong, because money exerts a *powerful* tug on every one of us, and we need to address it.

Recently as I read through the ancient book of Proverbs I simply marked on a pad of paper each verse that applied in some way to money. Total count was 80 verses. Someone has apparently done the same thing with the whole Bible claiming it contains approx. 2,350 verses about money. Why? Why would God be so concerned about a topic we consider so secular? It's obvious isn't it? It's not secular at all. The tug of money is a force exerted on each of our hearts.

Catch a glimpse of the power of money.

Proverbs 6:1-3 *"My son, if you have put up security for your neighbor, if you have shaken hands in pledge for a stranger, you have been trapped by what you said, ensnared by the words of your mouth. So do this, my son, to free yourself, since you have fallen into your neighbor's hands: Go – to the point of exhaustion – and give yourself no rest!"* Refuse to sleep until you get free of this commitment because a financial commitment controls your life.

Proverbs 15:27 *"The greedy bring ruin to their households…"* It is so strong it can bring the whole family down.

Proverbs 22:7, you've heard this one before: *"The rich rule over the poor, and the borrower is slave to the lender."* You want to talk about power; the Bible says you become an actual slave. Written in this decade he might say, "I owe, I owe so off to work I go."

Other Proverbs talk about not wearing yourself out to chase after money because it grows wings and flies away. Encouraging isn't it? Don't forget, most of these Proverbs were written by Solomon, one of the richest men ever, and while they each deal with a specific issue, taken together they make an even stronger point: *Money is a POWERFUL force.*

You say, "Not for me because I don't have much." Something I've learned over time is that the amount one possesses has almost nothing to do with how big an influence money has on them.

I spoke recently with a student who told me he didn't want a good bike to ride to school because if he had a good bike, he'd be worried someone would steal it. He was aware of the power of stuff. I've seen older folk who have lived frugally and have more than enough money, but they are so afraid to spend any of it they'll miss a necessary doctor's appointment before they will take a taxi and they'll do without proper medicine because it costs too much. Think of the powerful hold money has over them.

How about you?

Second, determine that your use of money reflects your most deeply held values. In other words, make sure there is no disconnect between your money and your beliefs.

Proverbs doesn't knock money. What it does is foster a healthy view of it. There's a whole series of Proverbs I love that are written in the format of "Better Than" statements. "Better is A than B." "Better Than" statements are value statements. Here are a few:

Proverbs 17:1 "*Better a dry crust with peace and quiet than a house full of feasting, with strife.*" You are better with cold toast, in peace, than you are with riches, and trouble.

Proverbs 15:17, I don't like this one, it's the vegetarians Proverb: "*Better a small serving of vegetables with love than a fattened calf with hatred.*" The fattened calf is a symbol of abundance, the ability to put on a feast with an animal prepared just for the occasion. He says you're better off eating a can of pork and beans, without the pork, with someone you love, than filet mignon and all the trimmings, accompanied by hate and bitterness.

Better than. Make financial decisions, he says, based on "better than" values. Here's the reality. Many of us make financial decisions and then wind up having to fit life around the demands those decisions impose. For example, someone buys too much house, with too huge a mortgage, in order to have a great place for the family to live. Then, both parents wind up working overtime in order to pay for it, so the family never spends any time together enjoying the house. As a result, their higher value of "home" gets sacrificed for the lesser value of "house." Proverbs says, determine not to do that. Make sure your use of money reflects what you really believe.

Recently Arlene and I were driving a few blocks from my office when a car passed us proudly displaying a beautiful pink ribbon magnet. As you know, it was promoting a "Cure For Breast Cancer." But as the car with the pink ribbon passed us, I couldn't help but notice that the driver was a young lady and in her hand was a cigarette. I don't get that. There she was; a moving advertisement for Cure for Cancer, while smoking. Her inconsistency hit mine right between the eyes. Make the determination that what you really value will be reflected in the way you handle money.

Third, determine to determine your financial course. I know that is clumsy English but try to grasp it. Determine to determine your course, make a plan, take full responsibility for it and stick with it, by the hour!

Proverbs 6:6 *"Go to the ant, you sluggard; consider its ways and be wise! It has no commander, no overseer or ruler, yet it stores its provisions in summer and gathers its food at harvest."* Even the ant has a savings plan.

You might wonder why I used such a strong word—determination. The answer is quite simple: financial responsibility is swimming upstream. We are bombarded every hour of every day with information that tells us we not only need, but we deserve more and more stuff. It's essential to be happy, we're told. Furthermore, many of our closest friends believe the lie and pursue it, leaving us odd man out if we elect not to comply. Navigating the $ forest will require every ounce of discipline and determination you have. So apply the hour by hour approach to it, and win the battle one dollar at a time.

Fourth, determine to share. Few practices slay the financial dragon more quickly or surely than generosity. Proverbs is full of verses describing what really occurs when God's people share.

Proverbs 19:17 *"Those who are kind to the poor lend to the Lord..."* Proverbs 11:24 ff, *"Whoever refreshes others will be refreshed."*

Let me tell you what sharing is not, because I think there's room for misunderstanding. Sharing isn't a good old fashioned church pot-luck dinner where we all bring a few dishes so we can all over indulge. Sharing is inviting a family over or taking a family out for dinner who would never get invited over or taken out, because they could never afford to pay you back. And you intentionally give them the best meal they'll have all month.

Sharing isn't going out on your boat and agreeing to meet six other friends with boats so you can have a flotilla and share the afternoon. Sharing is identifying a youngster from a financially strapped home and taking him or her out for an afternoon on your boat and teaching him to water ski knowing that when you do it may very well be the only boat ride this kid will ever get in his or her childhood.

Sharing isn't swapping your motorcycle with a friend for his Sea Doo for an afternoon of variety. Sharing is noticing a single mom or family at your kids' school driving a $1400 mini-van with bald tires and putting a good set of safe new tires on it for the winter. Remember I'm from Canada where it snows. Sharing is paying the registration and buying hockey or soccer equipment for the kid across town who dreams of the game as much as any kid anywhere but who will never play because it just costs too much. Sharing is educating yourself to realities around the world and doing without a few things so that children and their parents who are loved by Our Father in Heaven can have clean water to drink and some food to eat. And best of all, sharing is making sure ministries are fully resourced so people can have the ultimate gift, the message of the gospel of Jesus Christ.

You can tell without any doubt when you're finally beginning to really share because it will start to cost you; you'll deny yourself perks and pleasures you would normally consume in order to meet those kinds of needs … AND YOU WOULDN'T HAVE IT ANY OTHER WAY!!!

When you are at that point you have become the master of money and destroyed its power over you. You have also started living like Jesus.

Let's be very clear, sharing like that doesn't just happen. It's something you learn and grow into one hour at a time.

Stop The Clock

Without question it's true. Our actions clearly demonstrate our values. So here's the challenge:

1. *For one week record everything you spend – every single penny. (I know, it's a major pain, but very worthwhile)*

2. *During the course of the week attempt to be in touch with how you feel about your spending habits and what they reveal about you.*

3. *At the end of the week face the truth. Were there any surprises? Are you pleased with the places your money goes?*

4. *What adjustments do you want to make?*

CHAPTER TWENTY THREE
Maintaining Sexual North

Sex is often referred to as "the facts of life."
Well, the facts of life are that those things with the
capacity to bring the greatest pleasure also have
the capacity to bring the greatest pain.

Have you ever had a great idea, declared you were going to do it, but then, when it came time to follow through it was so overwhelming it made you wonder, "What in the world was I thinking?" Writing a chapter on human sexuality fits in that category. It seemed like such a good idea six months ago. Everyone struggles with their sexuality to some extent. How could I write a book about life and not include any mention of sex? But actually putting my thoughts down in black and white for you to read cause me to wonder what I was thinking. The task is even more daunting since I have no clue who might read these words.

Maybe you are single, and you're wondering, should I bother with this chapter? Is he just going to tell me how great sex can be in God's plan, and then say, but not for you? You must abstain. I heard of one speaker whose solution to that was to quote Napoleon Hill and tell the singles, "I'm afraid you are simply going to have to convert your sexual energy into other creative outlets like making money or promoting world peace." Not real helpful is it? I'll come back to you in a few minutes, but let me be clear; I think "maintaining sexual north" has a lot to say to you if you're single.

Maybe you are uncomfortable with this topic. You might be discussing this book in a small group and you really wish I hadn't included this chapter. I occasionally speak on sex in church and I often face this kind of response. There are some who always let me know they don't think sexual discussion is appropriate in church. They are so shy and conservative they think even the legs of the piano ought to be covered. And having a pastor talk about sex, in church, is really pushing the envelope.

Then, of course, there's the other end of the spectrum. There are those who are sex-obsessed. Sex is all they think about. There's a term for them too. They are called – men.

So with all these varying opinions floating around, why have I included this chapter? The answer really is quite simple and can be given in two words: Power and Confusion.

Few forces exert more power on our lives than the tug of human sexuality. Few issues have greater potential to either contribute to your happiness and satisfaction or to mess you up beyond belief. Get this one right and it can contribute to a healthy, happy, balanced life. But get it wrong and the damage it can do to your heart and to your loved ones is almost beyond description.

Word 2, confusion. Few forces are shrouded in more mystery and confusion than human sexuality. Few issues have the moral compass spinning more wildly out of control. In fact there is so much sexual confusion that doing any kind of statistical analysis of what is actually taking place is impossible. For example, some take comfort in the fact that several studies show that the level of teenage sexual activity is on the decline. However, just peel back the wrapping a little bit and you discover that ever since the Clinton era, "sexual activity" has been re-defined and anything less than full sexual intercourse doesn't register on most surveys. And truth is, far from a decline, 12 & 13 & 14 year old girls are wearing sexual bracelets where each color bead represents a different sexual activity they've been part of—and they wear them with pride. Some of them are tear-away beads and if a young guy at a party is able to tear away a bead, the girl has to engage in whatever sexual activity that color bead represents. That's reality for 13-year-olds today. And there is mass confusion about what's right or wrong and whether right and wrong has changed. I have simply reached the conclusion that if not even pastors are willing to hold the moral compass high, who will?

So, married or single, male or female, young or old, conservative or not so conservative, we need to talk. This subject is just too powerful and confusing to ignore.

Proverbs chapter 5 is a clear, concise talk from a father to his son about sex. Ladies, don't be put off by the male language, since it is father to son it obviously approaches the subject from that perspective BUT the principles have no gender. I might add a warning: Proverbs 5 is explicit and graphic It describes the horrors of getting this wrong and in enticing language it depicts the joys of getting it right.

So far in this book I haven't asked you to do this, but maybe this would be a good time to go get your Bible if you have one and open it to this text. It might help you appreciate what's being said if you realize it comes straight from a part of the Bible written thousands upon thousands of years ago. Proverbs 5 lays out a sexual battle plan (I know, those are tough words, but this issue is that powerful), a sexual battle plan that will enable you to optimize God's gift of sexuality.

Most battles are fought in stages, so here we go:

Stage 1: Adopt An End Result Mindset. Are you with me? Learn to ask yourself, "If I follow this path, where will I end up and is it where I want to end up?"

Verse 1 *My son, pay attention to my wisdom, turn your ear to my words of insight, that you may maintain discretion and your lips may preserve knowledge.*

He is just setting the stage, like any parent saying; listen up, I've got something important to say.

Verse 3 *For the lips of the adulterous woman drip honey, and her speech is smoother than oil; but in the end (key words) in the end she is bitter as gall, sharp as a double-edged sword.*

She looks, or since this is genderless, he appears so smooth, so enticing, like honey, but in the end, she's as bitter as gall. Some translations of the ancient words read, "She's as bitter as wormwood." Apparently it is shrub that grows in the area with an extremely bitter taste. She promises honey but winds up as vinegar.

The key phrase is, "in the end." She starts out looking like one thing, he starts out promising one thing, *but in the end* it turns out to be something quite different. It's one of Proverbs favorite phrases. Chapter 5:11 speaks of "at the end of your life." Chapter 14:12 is a repeated proverb that reminds us that there's a path that seems right, but in the end – death! Chapter 23 uses the phrase to describe the result of too much drinking. It starts out smooth but in the end it bites like a snake

The dad in this text says to his son, "You've got to have an end game mindset to keep you from being trapped by momentary allurements that simply do not and can not deliver what they promise." Do you want wormwood and vinegar or do you want to wind up years from now with verse 18 describing your life, *"May your fountain be blessed, and may you rejoice in the wife of your youth.*

When I was in University I worked for a grocery chain. In one of the stores I worked in we had a really nice assistant manager. He was warm and friendly and treated us extremely well. So you can imagine my surprise when I went to work one day and was told he'd just been fired. I could hardly believe it and asked the obvious question: Why? Apparently, customers would bring in pop bottles and pop cans. If they had $1.90 in bottle returns, the assistant manager would write cut the slip for $1.90, have the customer sign it, give them their money and then take his pen and turn the 1 into a 7. The other $6 would go directly into his pocket. Word was it gave him three, $2 bets on the ponies up at Northlands. He was so skilled he could also turn 3's into 8's. Someone higher up noticed that our store was doing an extraordinarily booming business in pop bottle returns and decided an audit was in order and for $5 here and there worth of pop bottles our boss lost a $90 thousand dollar a year job (or however much he made). We all just went: dumb, dumb. dumb.

You have got to think end game. You got to think big picture. Where do I want to end up? Will this path get me there, or in the end, will it turn to wormwood. Will the road I'm about to enter result in me celebrating 50 or 60 years of great marriage with my spouse or will I wind up alone in an empty basement suite after a series of one night stands, my spouse gone and my kids despising me?

Stage 1: adopt an end result mindset.

Stage 2: Recognize and Deal With Diversionary Influences.

This is a battle plan so I'm using military language very much on purpose. If you know where you want to wind up you've got to eliminate anything that will take you off that course.

Derek Kidner, one of my favorite authors on Proverbs says Proverbs 5 is largely about the fact that ***unwise sexual practice <u>dissipates irrevocably</u> the powers you've been given to invest.*** You only have so much of yourself to give and if you squander it, you wind up not being able to fully give yourself to the one you really love.

Notice some of what you lose in sexual infidelity. Verse 7: *Now then, my sons, listen to me; do not turn aside from what I say. Keep to a path far from her, do not go near the door of her house, lest you lose <u>your honor</u> to others and <u>your dignity</u> to one who is cruel.* Your honor and dignity, gone. Just ask anyone who has walked that path, they'll tell you, it's true.

Verse 12: *You will say, how I hated discipline! How my heart spurned correction! I would not obey my teachers or turn my ear to my instructors and soon I was in serious trouble in the assembly of God's people.*

I gave in to the diversions, I followed the lesser path, and where did it get me? I lost honor, I lost dignity, I got in trouble with the people who mattered most to me.

A few minutes ago I asked you to go get a Bible. Now I have another assignment for you. Find a dime and place it on the page in front of you. Got it? I know some of you are thinking you've got a lot more than 10 cents worth of sexual capital. Of course you do, but this is just a sample. It represents what you have to give.

Here's how the math works. You find the mate of your dreams and you spend a lifetime investing your sexual capital with him or her. You give yourselves fully and completely to each other and you enjoy human sexuality at its highest level. Dime with Dime.

But, let's say one of you chooses to engage in some innocent flirtation at work. (I'm not sure there is such a thing as innocent flirtation. Life is not an event it's a path. It heads in a specific direction. So, while your flirtation in and of itself may be innocent, it points you in a direction away from your spouse, that's the danger). You engage in that flirtation and you spend some of your sexual capital. Not much, maybe only a penny.

You go home that evening to your spouse and he or she presents you with their dime and you say, "You bet, you can have all of me." But guess what? All of you is only *9 cents* because you spent one at the office. Now you've got a sexual relationship that's unequal. It's barely noticeable at first, but your union is not 100% complete. If you've been there and I suspect most of us have, you know what I'm talking about. It's not disastrous, it's just one penny short.

But then you engage in some pornography, allowing your mind and your focus and your attention to go down that path and you spend 3 more pennies. You then go to your spouse that evening and he or she presents you with their dime, and in turn you say, "You bet, you can have all of me." But all of you is now only **6 *pennies*** because you spent 1 flirting and 3 on the computer. By this point the impact on your sexual relationship is noticeable. It's not fulfilling at all because it's a dime with six pennies.

Or, much more common today, BOTH PARTNERS HAVE SPENT CHANGE ELSEWHERE!!! So instead of the ultimate relationship, dime with dime, you've got 7¢ with 5¢, and you're wondering, where did the magic go? You spent it!

I don't think I need to play this out any further; an affair takes a ton of change out of any relationship.

Singles, I said I'd come back to you. I know it seems hard, but if you squander your sexual capital with whomever, whenever, however, all along the way, you simply will have less to offer the one you really love and want to commit the rest of your life to when you find them..

Now, please, please pay very close attention. I need to take this in two different directions. First, to those of you who are broken or wounded sexually and who right this moment have a very sick feeling in the pit of your stomach because you can see exactly what you've done. You need to know of the redeeming grace of the Lord Jesus Christ Who will forgive you and enable you to get on the right path and begin putting pennies back into your account. It won't be easy, it's a long journey, but the Bible is clear, "though your sins were red like crimson, He can wash you whiter than snow." If you need to, take that step with Him today, confess to Him, claim His forgiveness and walk the road of redemption and re-deposit wholeness back into your sexual life, one hour at a time.

However, and I want to be so careful here, to you who know better, who know you're on the wrong path and are continuing down it anyway. To those who think it's no big deal if you mess up sexually because God forgives. If you are on that track, yes if you sincerely repent God will forgive you. However, you will have still spent capital that you know you've spent and the person you spent it with knows you've spent. Some of that capital takes years to recover (like your dignity and honor) and some of it you can never recover (like your virginity which you can only give once).

So please, adopt an end result mindset and then be vigilant and ruthless about any diversionary influences that will take you away from that goal. From this day forward make it your goal to present your spouse with a whole dime, each and every day.

All right, take a deep breath the negative part is over, let's get positive.

Stage 3: Pursue Passionate Fidelity. Pursue it, build it and fully enjoy it.

A while back I was flying into Kelowna and my seat mates on the airplane were from Saskatchewan. They were coming to tour wineries. We looked out the window and commented on the beautiful valley and lake and they began asking all sorts of questions. I enquired if this was their first visit to our area and they said, "No, we came last year too." They warmed to the topic and said, "We had a great time last year. In fact we know a guy who owns a boat dealership. One of the highlights of our trip was when we went to his boat place and climbed onto one of those patio boats right there beside the highway and opened a bottle of wine. We took out our lunch and had a wonderful picnic, on the boat."

I tried my best to contain myself and not laugh out loud. They picnicked in a boat in a parking lot beside the highway and thought it was great. They really were from Saskatchewan. (Sorry, I promised myself, no Saskatchewan jokes in this book but that was just too easy). Trying to cover my laughter I said to them, "How about this year you live on the edge a bit and try it ... on the water!"

This is now truth time. The truth is that sexually many couples have never gotten out of the boat yard. If you want to affair-proof your marriage, if you want the best, you have to go for it. Don't settle. Men, she's around sharp executives all day who are crisp and who mind their manners and treat her with respect and sensitivity. If you show up belching in your sweats ... Gals, come on, if you want the best, be your best and try your best. You both deserve it.

Proverbs is far more explicit than most pastors usually get. First, it gives the exhortation in verse 15 to *drink water from your own cistern, running water from your own well.* Then he really gets going and says, "Cistern? Well water? Forget it." *May your fountain, (your FOUNTAIN) be blessed, and may you rejoice in the wife of your youth, a loving doe, a graceful deer, may her breasts satisfy you always, may you ever be intoxicated with her love.* You're to be intoxicated, captivated, exhilarated by sexual thoughts of your spouse, right down to specific body parts. That simply won't happen unless you pursue it and put a little energy and creativity into it.

One of the biggest and most under-rated factors in an electric sex life is respect. Nothing turns people on or off more quickly or certainly than respect or loss of it. So, I throw out the challenge to all married couples to notch it up a bit and be at your very best with your spouse and pursue passionate fidelity.

Stage 4: Annihilate Secrecy.

After the fun of Stage 3, this one is a rather sobering stage. If I could make only one statement about how to maintain sexual north, this would be it. Most sexual damage is done in secret, and all it would take to keep most of us on course, is to get rid of the secrecy.

Verse 21 *For your ways are in full view of the Lord, and he examines all your paths.*

Remember the context, this is father to son, having the "sex talk" and he says, son, remember, nothing ultimately is secret.

Here's what I'm not saying. I'm not saying you have to go back and unearth every sordid detail of your life. Sometimes that does more damage than good. But, as of today … just drive a stake in the ground, and say**, no more secrets.** I am going to live my life open and above board.

Here's one example of what that might look like.

www.x3watch.com

That website is for any of you who are spending your sexual capital on internet pornography and want to be set free. You've promised God over and over but you keep going back. Why, because it's so easy to do in secret and the secrecy is killing you. You go to that website and follow the prompts and it will ask you to enter the addresses of 2 or 3 accountability partners and from that point on, any time you access a pornographic site on your computer your accountability partners will receive an email telling them and you can expect a conversation. It's all about accountability.

That's an example of the kind of thing that can help you maintain sexual north by annihilating secrecy.

Remember, the facts of life are that *those things with the capacity to bring the greatest pleasure also have the capacity*

to bring the greatest pain. Make sure you win this battle every single hour.

Stop The Clock

This chapter contains both challenge and encouragement for everyone, regardless your marital status. The questions are extremely basic.

1. *Is there anything in your life you need to stop in order to maintain Sexual North? Are you spending your sexual capital in areas where it will not bring God's blessed return?*

2. *Are there things you need to begin in order to maximize your sexuality? Have you been taking this precious gift for granted and assigning only left-over energy or uncreative routine to it? What can you do to appropriately spice up your life in this area?*

CHAPTER TWENTY FOUR
Your Most Important Hour

Every prodigal needs to know only one truth ...
... he can go home!

How long has it been since you've wrestled with fear? I don't mean a sudden, adrenaline-jolting fear like you get when someone jumps out from behind a wall and goes, "Boo," but fear that grabs you and envelopes you and makes your heart race and palms sweat.

I recently traveled to Chicago for a personal, spiritual retreat. I had some time before the retreat started so I went to a White Sox baseball game. If you know Chicago you know that the White Sox play on the south side in an area that is "challenging." For a small town Canadian those "challenges" are quite fear-inducing. I found my way to the ball park but somehow missed the main parking lot and wound up in one of those little "side ventures."

I'm sure I was perfectly safe but my fear took over and I started imagining things. As I walked down the street all by myself, toward the stadium, a great big fellow smoking a cigar and wearing lots of rings on his fingers called out to me in a deep, raspy voice. He said, "You goin the wrong way, brotha." I kept going, eyes straight ahead, my pace on the quick side. He called again, "I'm telling ya, you goin the wrong way to the ballpark." Finally, after the third call, I turned around and noticed he was grinning and he pointed to a narrow little alley between two buildings and said, "You need to go through there, otherwise it's seven blocks around."

As I looked down that little alley, a Bible verse came to mind. It was, "Yea though I walk through the alley of the shadow of death," and seven blocks didn't seem so far. While I hesitated, he crossed the street and came right up to me. He got real close and said, "I'm just trying to save you a walk and since I helped you maybe you can help me. I'm from the Children's Ministry of that church over there and we could use a little donation."

The first thought that crossed my mind was, "If I get out of this alive, I'm going to try to get a few ushers at my church just like this guy." He knew how to get people to give.

That night the opening line in my journal was, "I prayed more than usual today." I don't mind telling you, I was scared.

As I described my experience did you observe anything other than the sad fact that I'm a coward? Did you notice the by-products of fear?

- How it made me suspicious?
- How it made me rude?

- Did you notice that it led me to prefer to walk seven blocks around rather than directly to the park?

- Did you notice that it sucked the joy out of what should have been a great moment?

All this from one little fear! But it was a fear that controlled my life.

For 23 chapters we've talked about a strategy to ensure that that doesn't happen in areas of life that matter most. We've discussed how to not only survive life's challenges, but to flourish. Throughout our dialogue I've quoted liberally from the Bible and have made a major assumption that now, in this closing chapter I want to clarify. I've assumed that you know God. That you and He are on speaking terms and that He leads and guides your life. I have assumed that you are more like Oscar, who on his death bed talked intimately with his God than you are like the young man in the garage who could find no reason to go on living. The problem is I don't know if my assumption about you and your relationship with God is accurate. So, as I write the closing chapter I want to describe how it can be. I want you to know that you can have that kind of intimate relationship with your God.

Let's forego beating around the bush and get right to the core issue of an authentic, flourishing life. *The core issue is the power of*

I've assumed that you know God. That you and He are on speaking terms and that He leads and guides your life.

the grace of God to deal with whatever is holding you back (primarily and specifically the sin that has scarred you) and to engage you in a reason to live. Both halves of the equation are vital. For years some Christians have taught that Christianity is primarily to equip people to die. They have asked people to confess their sins and to invite Jesus to be their Saviour, so that they'll be ready to die – period. The problem is they've given people a faith to die for but nothing to live for. The core issue of an authentic, flourishing life is the power of the grace of God to deal with your past to such an extent that you are empowered to live each and every present hour fully. As it says in the Lord's Prayer, you become a partner to build His Kingdom on earth as it is in heaven.

I recently heard this deep theological truth expressed from a most unlikely source, from an NHL coach. Commenting on the poor performance of one of his very highly paid players, the coach said, "We viewed his signing of the big contract as the beginning, he obviously viewed it as the end." Getting right with God is not primarily a deathbed move, it's preparation to really live.

Observe with me several factors that are just true about this life-changing partnership with God. The factors I want you to observe are found in those incredible stories about real life told by Jesus, and recorded in the *Gospel of Luke chapter 15*. You've probably heard them before so they won't be foreign to you. Observe closely.

The first observation I want you to make is that the obstacles that keep us from surviving and flourishing come in all varieties of colors, shapes and sizes. There is no one formula for failure.

Luke 15 contains three stories which are drastically different from each other. I'm convinced they're different on purpose. Jesus told back to back to back stories, each about being lost, but as different from each other as night and day, to make the point that there is no one stereotype of person who's lost and in need of God. We all fit these stories somewhere.

Story #1 features a lost sheep. *Suppose one of you has a hundred sheep and loses one of them ...*

How does that happen? We all know. The grass looks just a little greener a few feet away. The shade appears a little cooler, so the sheep wanders just a bit, and then a bit more. It ducks behind that tree and thinks, "Look, there's another tuft of green, I may lay down here for a moment." The drifting is gentle and gradual but all of a sudden I (I mean the sheep) have drifted just far enough that I don't know how to get back. I'm lost.

A while back I was driving down one of our city's busiest streets when I saw a dog running down the middle of the road. You've seen that crazed, panicked look of a lost dog in the middle of traffic. It's haunting. It's a bewildered, confused, scared look. And of course it's a look of abject loneliness. The 99 sheep were together but a feature of the lost sheep is always that it is alone and afraid.

Is that you?

Story #2 is about the lost coin. *"Or suppose a woman has ten silver coins and loses one ..."*

I came across an interesting explanation of her loss. An observer commented on how big a deal it was that this lady had managed to save ten coins. Perhaps it was her security for the future. Maybe it was for her pilgrimage. Or possibly, as one historian suggested, girls in that day would save up coins and make them into a necklace or bracelet which would be their bridal preparation, their hope chest, and this poor gal had finally managed to scrounge up ten coins, the symbol of her hope and future when suddenly the table got bumped and it was gone. And in the dusty, dirt floor culture she lit the lamp and swept the entire area, desperate because she was looking for her shattered dream.

If you've been in those shoes you don't need me to tell you what that does to your self esteem. Just ask any 55-year-old wife who got traded in for a 39-year-old; or perhaps for pictures and videos of a 25-year-old; or ask a 55-year-old executive who just got cut free for a youth movement; or a young person who's always dreamed of becoming something but just can't seem to make it; or a senior who's been bumped off the table so many times no one bothers to look anymore. After enough bumps we don't even try to get up any more. We just lay there in the dust.

Story #3 is the most tragic. *"Jesus continued, 'There was a man who had two sons. The younger one said to his father...'"* you know the story. "Give me my inheritance. I'm tired of waiting for you to die." Imagine THAT conversation! *"Not long after that, the younger one got together all he had, set off for a distant country and there squandered his wealth in wild living. After he had spent everything, there was a severe famine in that whole country, and he began to be in need."*

Don't read that too quickly. Remember we're trying to observe truth in it. When did this son get lost? We usually focus on the phrase, and it's a great phrase, "after he had spent everything." It seems clear that then he's bankrupt, lost, and in despair. But think it through and I think you'll agree with me, he was just as lost a week or a month or three months before the cash ran out. The cash just masked his lost-ness a bit longer.

I'm camping here intentionally because most of us think that if the cash hasn't run out yet everything and everyone's okay. People look good. Nice job, nice neighborhood, nice this, nice that ... but it's all smoke and mirrors.

Sound familiar?

Three stories as different as can be, with one common denominator: they each describe a horrible lost-ness. It serves to raise the question, "If you see yourself in there, what are you going to do about it? Are you going to cover-up and hide, or will you allow yourself to be found?"

Some hide by making their lost-ness somebody else's fault. There's someone to blame, maybe society, maybe my parents, maybe the church, maybe those hypocrites. Others hide by giving up and withdrawing. Some, like the prodigal, hide by masking it with fast living, or immersing themselves in work, or any of a multitude of addictions.

In Luke 15 Jesus went to the wall to get us to face the truth about our lost-ness, to get us to be authentic about our condition.

So, I'm asking, "Do you see yourself anywhere in here?" I can tell you in all honesty that at various stages in my life I've been in all three stories. Where are you this hour?

Having honesty answered that question, let's keep observing. The second observation I want to point out from these stories is that regardless where you find yourself, God is aggressively pursuing you. I love this part. God is not passive, waiting for you to come to your senses. He's aggressively looking for you and pursuing you. Often when we're lost we think God is against us, or out to get us, or at best, that He's neutral, waiting for me to get my act together. But you can't read these three stories without realizing that God is not only not against you, He's not even neutral. He's aggressively pursuing you.

Read on. "*Suppose one of you has a hundred sheep and loses one of them. Doesn't he leave the ninety-nine in the open country and go after the lost sheep until he finds it?*"

One scholar writing on this story says that when the shepherds would come in from the fields at night the community would be watching. They couldn't tell if one sheep was missing. What they would notice was that a shepherd was missing, and everyone would know, he's out searching. The crucial phrase in this story is that "*he goes after the lost sheep ... until he finds it.*"

"*Or suppose a woman has ten silver coins and loses one of them. Doesn't she light a lamp, sweep the house and search carefully until she finds it?*" She's not sweeping the floor for cleanliness reasons. She's on a mission and she will not stop until she fulfills it.

And you know the story of the prodigal's father. It's one of the most moving scenes in scripture. "*But while he (the prodigal) was still a long way off, his father saw him and was filled with compassion for him; he ran to his son, threw his arms around him and kissed him.*" Any parent with a wayward child understands this completely. How did he see him a long way off? Answer: he was out there looking, watching, straining, and he saw the form, recognized the unique gait and did what fathers in that culture would never do, wrapped his robe around him and ran with all he had.

Pay very close attention to this. Jesus told not one, not two, but three stories so that you couldn't possibly miss how His Father, the Heavenly Father, feels about you. No matter if you are lost or hiding or broken or running or crushed or bewildered or filled with despair or searching for meaning, He always takes the first step toward you, His hand is always outstretched. In fact I believe in these stories Jesus was giving a clue about the extreme the Father would go to for you, He was thinking ahead to His own love-motivated death on a cross that would deal with all the blame and guilt to bridge the gap back to God. As hard as it may be to believe, God wants to enjoy an authentic relationship with you so much, Jesus died to make it possible.

Observation three is such a cool part of the story. I really want you to observe that there is no such thing as partial redemption. There are no second rate members of God's family.

A while back a hotel chain sent me a gold, honors membership card on a one year free trial basis. It included all kinds of little bonuses and perks. I used it a couple times, and it was great. I'd show up at their hotel and I'd be greeted by name, there'd be a little snack or gift or something waiting in my room. It was awesome. But, they quickly found out, I'm not nearly a valuable enough customer to justify that kind of treatment, so recently I got a letter from them telling me that unfortunately I had not quite met the standards of their Gold Card status, so they were canceling it and sending me my new Blue card. They expressed hope that I'd continue to frequent their hotels. I looked at that Blue card and immediately started to mope and complain to Arlene about the fact that I got kicked out of their gold club.

That's exactly how most of us have been conditioned to think about how God views us. We don't really matter. We're not VIP's. We're second class. We're blue card. We don't fit with the Billy Graham's and Mother Theresa's of this world. Sure, maybe God will take us to heaven when we die, if we're not too bad, but that's about it.

And nothing could be further from the truth!

Verse 5 *"When he finds it (the lost sheep) he joyfully puts it on his shoulders and goes home. Then he calls his friends and neighbors together and says, 'Rejoice with me; I have found my lost sheep.'"* On his shoulders, on his shoulders he carries that dirty, smelly sheep and then when he gets home, he then throws a party.

Verse 9 *"And when she finds it, she calls her friends and neighbors together and says, 'Rejoice with me; I have found my lost coin.'"* She calls long distance and says, "Guess what? I found it. Rejoice!"

And best of all, best of all, the prodigal, who was going to hire on as the lowest day laborer on his fathers ranch, when his dad reached him all out of breath he said, *"Quick! Bring the best robe* (not just any robe) *and put it on him. Put a ring on his finger and sandals on his feet. Bring the fattened calf and kill it. Let's have a feast and celebrate."* My SON is home! Each of the actions is filled with meaning, the robe to replace his tattered garments, the ring, the symbol of authority and possession, the sandals, which only the children wore, not slaves, and the fattened calf being saved for a special occurrence.

> God has no second class children.

Jesus told stories to do everything He could to convince the lost and the critics alike that God has no second class children. There's no such thing as partial redemption. He calls you out of hiding, forgives your sin because of Jesus' death on the cross, and invites you to FULL membership in His family. It's not an invitation to just get you in heaven's door, it's an invitation to join the family business and to play a meaningful, life-giving role.

The only question is, whether or not YOU will accept His invitation, because ... *You have an Option.* He won't force you out of hiding and he won't force you to be found. He invites and he takes the first step but you have an option. And you can choose the *Adam Plan* and hide in the fig leaves and blame Eve and the snake and everyone else; or you can choose *The Prodigal Plan* and come home.

Now, let me be very clear and practical and specific. How do you do that? The prodigal gives a clear demonstration. He acknowledged his need of the Father's grace. He admitted his fault, accepted the Father's provision and returned home where, (the story assumes) he launched a new life under the Father's direction. It wasn't the end, it was a brand new beginning.

My friend Oscar lived that way and he died that way. So can you. With God as Your Heavenly Father and the Lord Jesus as your Saviour, you can not only *survive* but you can *flourish*, this, and every hour.

Stop The Clock

1. *Do any of the pictures of lost-ness describe you today?*

2. *Come to terms with how you truly feel about God. Do you see Him as against you, neutral, or pursuing you in love? Are you willing to dig into the Bible to find out how it pictures Him?*

3. *If you understand that the Father is openly inviting you to come back home, experience His forgiveness and engage fully in the family business, how do you respond?*

Notes

Chapter 1

Bob Buford, <u>Half Time</u> (Zondervan: Grand Rapids, 1994).

Laurie Beth Jones, <u>The Path</u> (Hyperion: New York, 1996).

Rick Warren, <u>Purpose Driven Life</u> (Zondervan: Grand Rapids, 2002).

Chapter 2

William James, cited in Robert Cooper, <u>The Other 90%</u> (Crown Business: New York, 2001).

Robert Cooper, <u>The Other 90%</u> (Crown Business: New York, 2001).

Chapter 10

Richard A. Swenson MD, <u>Margin</u> (NavPress: Colorado Springs, 2004).

Chapter 13

Eob Reccord and Randy Singer, <u>Made To Count</u> (W Publishing Group: Nashville, 2004).

Chapter 14

Gary Thomas, Sacred Pathways (Zondervan: Nashville, 2000)

Chapter 16

Billy Graham, <u>Peace With God</u> (Double Day: New York, 1953).